DR JEKYLL & MR HYDE

VOCABULARY

GUIDED STUDY WORKBOOK

KS4 English Literature

GCSE 9-1 Texts

ABOUT THIS GUIDED STUDY WORKBOOK

Developed for pupils in Years 10 & 11 studying *Dr Jekyll and Mr Hyde* for their GCSEs, this targeted workbook uses a **new approach** to guide students through the **complex language** in the novella, **focusing on the key words that students need to understand to master the text**.

Covering over **300 words essential** to unlocking *Dr Jekyll and Mr Hyde,* this workbook is made up of ten units. Each unit provides students with
- **Targeted lists** of words and their meanings (of no more than twenty at a time) to learn
- **Focused vocabulary exercises** to reinforce the meanings they have memorised and to test themselves
- **Varied question types** including
  - Matching words and meanings
  - Cloze tests
  - Identifying synonyms and antonyms
  - Exploring and building word associations
  - Locating and explaining words in context

This workbook also includes **10 extra *Jekyll & Hyde* Vocabulary Scavenger Hunt Challenges!**

Plus, for your convenience, this workbook contains
- Material suitable for **ALL UK exam boards including AQA, OCR & Edexcel**
- The **complete answers** to all the exercises & vocabulary scavenger hunts
- Two **complete lists** of all the target words and their meanings in this workbook organised by **(1) chapter** and **(2) alphabetical order**

HOW TO USE IT

THE UNITS
- Read the list of targeted words and meanings relating to the part of the novella you are concentrating on
- Identify the words that you're familiar with and the ones that you're not
- Learn the unfamiliar words
- Once you're confident you've mastered the target words, work through the exercises on the following pages
- Check your answers and, if needed, revise any meanings that haven't quite stuck

As the units are **self-contained**, you can either work through them **in order**, or use them for **focused practice** and/or **revision**. If you are new to the text, however, we recommend that you do the units in sequence.

THE VOCABULARY SCAVENGER HUNT CHALLENGES
- Each Challenge directs you to a particular section of the text for you to read carefully
- When you've done this, work through the list of clues provided to find a range of single words, phrases, sentences, & figures of speech

The Challenges target **over 100 words NOT included** in any of the units, so you can **attempt the Challenges at any point in time**.

Published by STP Books
An imprint of Swot Tots Publishing Ltd
Kemp House
152-160 City Road
London EC1V 2NX

www.swottotspublishing.com

Text, design, and layout © Swot Tots Publishing Ltd. First published 2021.

Swot Tots Publishing Ltd have asserted their moral right under the Copyright, Designs and Patents Act, 1988, to be identified as the author of this work.

Typeset, cover design, and inside concept design by Swot Tots Publishing Ltd.

British Library Cataloguing-in-Publication Data. A catalogue record for this book is available from the British Library.

ISBN 978-1-912956-34-0

CONTENTS

CONTENTS CONTINUED

DON'T FORGET!

*You can access our Free Online Jekyll & Hyde Quiz @ **http://bit.ly/3mNLWYX** & our Free Online Jekyll & Hyde Quotes Gallery @ **http://bit.ly/3hhHujL**. Alternatively, you can use the QR Codes provided on the back cover of this workbook.*

...AND, FINALLY, JUST BEFORE YOU DIVE IN...

Word Order: *The order of the target words in all the units of this workbook follow the order in which R. L. Stevenson uses them in each of the chapters. Each group of words is set out in two VERTICAL columns which should always be read starting from the topmost entry in the LEFT column.*

Definitions: *Language changes. Consequently, the meanings of the words provided in this workbook <u>reflect the ways Stevenson uses them</u>.*

Editions: *As a work of classic literature, numerous editions of the text are available. You may, therefore, occasionally encounter slight differences between your edition and the extracts in this workbook.*

GOOD LUCK!

UNIT 1: STORY OF THE DOOR

WORDS & MEANINGS ~ GROUP A

rugged: stony

countenance: face

dusty: uninteresting

eminently: extremely

beaconed: shone

austere: strict

mortify: suppress

vintages: expensive wines

heresy: unconventional opinion

chambers: office

catholicity: broad-mindedness

kinsman: relative

singularly: distinctly

chanced: happened

rambles: walks

emulously: competitively

in coquetry: attractively

thoroughfare: road

florid: flamboyant

passage: customers

WHERE TO FIND THEM

The above words appear in the following section of 'Story Of The Door':

From the START of the paragraph that begins with

Mr Utterson the lawyer was a man of a rugged countenance that was never lighted by a smile; cold, scanty and embarrassed in discourse...

to the END of the paragraph that begins with

It chanced on one of these rambles that their way led them down a by-street in a busy quarter of London. The street was...

BEFORE YOU START

Once you've reviewed the target words above, use this space to make a note of (i) all the words that you didn't know (before reading the meanings) and/or (ii) all the words you're uncertain about.

The words that you make a note of here are the words that you want to make sure that you've mastered by the time you get to the end of this part of the unit.

I.I Match the given words on the left to their correct meanings on the right. Then, use the letter to complete the definition statements below.

SAMPLE ANSWER: _Z_ is the meaning of **happy**

Words	Meanings
rugged	A. road
countenance	B. attractively
dusty	C. unconventional opinion
eminently	D. strict
beaconed	E. customers
austere	F. competitively
mortify	G. walks
vintages	H. uninteresting
heresy	I. distinctly
chambers	J. office
catholicity	K. expensive wines
kinsman	L. face
singularly	M. shone
chanced	N. relative
rambles	O. happened
emulously	P. extremely
in coquetry	Q. flamboyant
thoroughfare	R. suppress
florid	S. broad-mindedness
passage	T. stony

1. ___ is the meaning of **rugged**.

2. ___ is the meaning of **countenance**.

3. ___ is the meaning of **dusty**.

4. ___ is the meaning of **eminently**.

5. ___ is the meaning of **beaconed**.

6. ___ is the meaning of **austere**.

7. ___ is the meaning of **mortify**.

8. ___ is the meaning of **vintages**.

9. ___ is the meaning of **heresy**.

10. ___ is the meaning of **chambers**.

11. ___ is the meaning of **catholicity**.

12. ___ is the meaning of **kinsman**.

13. ___ is the meaning of **singularly**.

14. ___ is the meaning of **chanced**.

15. ___ is the meaning of **rambles**.

16. ___ is the meaning of **emulously**.

17. ___ is the meaning of **in coquetry**.

18. ___ is the meaning of **thoroughfare**.

19. ___ is the meaning of **florid**.

20. ___ is the meaning of **passage**.

1. Crossing the busy (beacon / thoroughfare / countenance), Mr Harris made his way to the bank.

2. The man's (chambers / vintages / countenance) bore the scars of some terrible injury.

3. "Lack of (thoroughfare / rambles / passage) has reduced our profit," the shopworker said.

4. Before the race began, the contestants eyed each other (eminently / in coquetry / emulously).

5. As it (chanced / beaconed / rugged), I bumped into the very person I'd planned to call.

6. In the cellar, they discovered racks upon racks of rare (vintages / heresies / thoroughfares).

7. Gary has worked hard to (austere / thoroughfare / mortify) his impulse to be sarcastic.

8. I found that horror film (ruggedly / emulously / singularly) disturbing.

9. The floral arrangements had been placed (emulously / heretically / in coquetry) in the hall.

10. Before us stood the (florid / rugged / beaconed) mountain, silent and unwelcoming.

11. "The mayor is a (vintage / countenance / kinsman) of mine," announced Olaf proudly.

12. Relief (beaconed / chanced / rambled) from all the faces of the rescued miners.

13. As he loves numbers, Otto is (floridly / emulously / eminently) suited to being an accountant.

14. Nina cringed at the (florid / austere / rugged) pink and yellow wallpaper in her new office.

15. The vizier was renowned for the (kinsman / catholicity / vintage) of his judgements.

16. Piya and her father have always enjoyed their countryside (catholicity / rambles / chambers).

17. "As an American, it's a bit of a (heresy / countenance / catholicity) to dislike baseball," Liv said.

18. The lawyer retired to his (thoroughfare / chambers / passage) to consider the matter further.

19. Sheila found the Regency novel she was reading quite (dusty / eminently / emulous).

20. While she can be (in coquetry / austere / vintage), our biology teacher is also fair.

1. **beaconed** | gestured   shone   extinguished   smoked

2. **vintages** | gifts   heirlooms   expensive wines   antiques

3. **chanced** | altered   happened   planned   imagined

4. **passage** | movements   progressions   customers   trades

5. **chambers** | auditorium   office   cell   vault

6. **singularly** | obliquely   distinctly   immorally   vaguely

7. **countenance** | build   tally   reverse   face

8. **dusty** | gripping   ancient   uninteresting   scholarly

9. **austere** | lax   strict   immoral   moral

10. **thoroughfare** | efficiency   via   well bred   road

11. **eminently** | extremely   immediately   repeatedly   slightly

12. **kinsman** | relative   acquaintance   companion   alter ego

13. **mortify** | soothe   enjoy   indulge   suppress

14. **catholicity** | broad-mindedness   extremism   intolerance   prejudice

15. **heresy** | orthodox opinion   theoretical opinion   unconventional opinion   dogmatic opinion

16. **in coquetry** | hopefully   seriously   arrogantly   attractively

17. **emulously** | conjointly   emotively   singularly   competitively

18. **rugged** | stony   carpeted   harmful   tender

19. **rambles** | walks   chats   thorns   complaints

20. **florid** | dull   unadorned   flamboyant   obese

UNIT I: STORY OF THE DOOR

WORDS & MEANINGS ~ GROUP B

passenger: pedestrian

gable: upper triangular-shaped part of a wall

distained: discoloured

mouldings: decorations

ravages: damage

cane: walking stick

Juggernaut: unstoppable force

collared: grabbed

Sawbones: doctor

apothecary: doctor

harpies: angry women

screwed: forced

apocryphal: doubtful

proprieties: respectability

capers: mischief

vein: mood

delicacy: reluctance

partakes too much of: has too much in common with

Queer Street: financial difficulties

pedantically: excessively

WHERE TO FIND THEM

The above words appear in the following section of 'Story Of The Door':

From the START of the paragraph that begins with

It chanced on one of these rambles that their way led them down a by-street in a busy quarter of London. The street was...

to the START of the paragraph that begins with

"I think you might have warned me," returned the other with a touch of sullenness. "But I have been pedantically exact, as you call it...

BEFORE YOU START

Once you've reviewed the target words above, use this space to make a note of (i) all the words that you didn't know (before reading the meanings) and/or (ii) all the words you're uncertain about.

The words that you make a note of here are the words that you want to make sure that you've mastered by the time you get to the end of this part of the unit.

I.4 Read the definition statements below and decide whether each is correct or incorrect. If the definition is correct, mark it with a capital 'T'. If it is incorrect, mark it with a capital 'F'.

1. The word **Juggernaut** means **unstoppable force**.   _____

2. The word **harpies** means **doubtful**.   _____

3. The word **ravages** means **damage**.   _____

4. The word **screwed** means **excessively**.   _____

5. The word **delicacy** means **angry women**.   _____

6. The word **proprieties** means **has too much in common with**.   _____

7. The word **cane** means **walking stick**.   _____

8. The words **partakes too much of** mean **financial difficulties**.   _____

9. The word **apocryphal** means **mood**.   _____

10. The word **Sawbones** means **doctor**.   _____

11. The word **capers** means **forced**.   _____

12. The word **apothecary** means **doctor**.   _____

13. The word **collared** means **grabbed**.   _____

14. The word **gable** means **upper triangular-shaped part of a wall**.   _____

15. The words **Queer Street** mean **respectability**.   _____

16. The word **distained** means **discoloured**.   _____

17. The word **mouldings** means **decorations**.   _____

18. The word **vein** means **mischief**.   _____

19. The word **pedantically** means **reluctance**.   _____

20. The word **passenger** means **pedestrian**.   _____

I.5 Build a Word Web of your associations with each of the words supplied in the following diagrams. The labels in each of the boxes have been provided to help guide your thoughts. Add more links and boxes of your own if you think of them!

SAMPLE ANSWER:

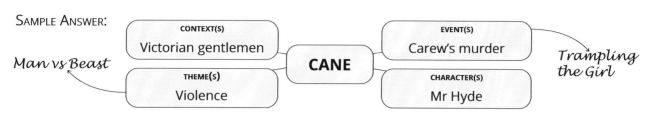

Man vs Beast

CONTEXT(S)
Victorian gentlemen

CANE

EVENT(S)
Carew's murder

Trampling the Girl

THEME(S)
Violence

CHARACTER(S)
Mr Hyde

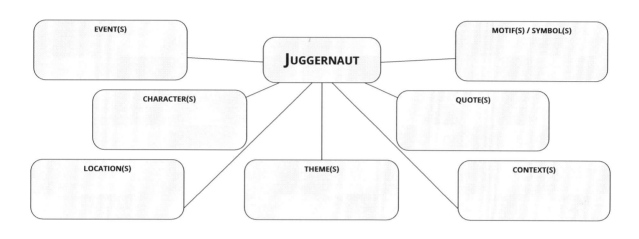

JUGGERNAUT

EVENT(S)

MOTIF(S) / SYMBOL(S)

CHARACTER(S)

QUOTE(S)

LOCATION(S)

THEME(S)

CONTEXT(S)

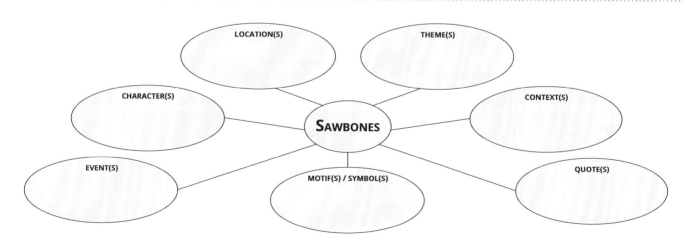

SAWBONES

LOCATION(S)

THEME(S)

CHARACTER(S)

CONTEXT(S)

EVENT(S)

MOTIF(S) / SYMBOL(S)

QUOTE(S)

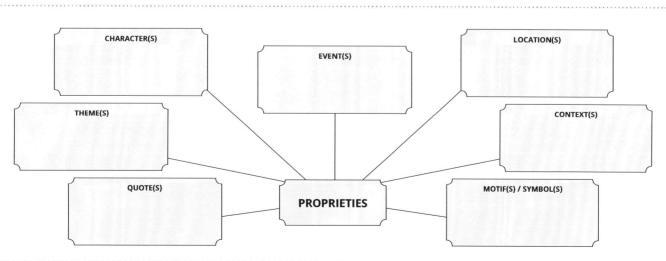

PROPRIETIES

CHARACTER(S)

EVENT(S)

LOCATION(S)

THEME(S)

CONTEXT(S)

QUOTE(S)

MOTIF(S) / SYMBOL(S)

1. I peered up at the (capers / delicacy / gable), trying to see what Jessie was pointing at.

2. The young thief narrowly escaped the group of (ravages / harpies / capers) pursuing him.

3. As ever, Melinda's final report was (pedantically / apocryphally / disdainfully) detailed.

4. It was in a solemn (gable / caper / vein) that the townspeople arrived at the meeting.

5. "You'd best call a (juggernaut / sawbones / harpy)," advised Jarvis. "That lad don't look well."

6. The pommel of my grandfather's (cane / caper / apothecary) was made of brass.

7. As we walked through the town, the (canes / ravages / sawbones) of the war shocked us.

8. The (passenger / apothecary / juggernaut) took down several jars of herbs from a shelf.

9. "Such behaviour (distains / canes / partakes too much of) unlawfulness," intoned the judge.

10. "It is with much (delicacy / collar / moulding) that I mention this," stated Lord Pomeroy.

11. I've always loved the (proprieties / sawbones / mouldings) that adorn our front door.

12. Sadly, Mr Bumble found himself on (Juggernaut Street / Queer Street / Pedant Street).

13. "As a boy, I was often disciplined for my (capers / gables / passengers)," Sanjay recalled.

14. Racing down the street, Emilia almost collided with a fellow (passenger / gable / delicacy).

15. The trouble with white towels is that they become (screwed / distained / collared) easily.

16. "The (canes / proprieties / gables) of society must be maintained!" declared Lady Bracknell.

17. It is a shame that anecdote is (delicate / apocryphal / collared); it is highly entertaining!

18. Eric (collared / distained / gabled) me as I tried to sneak out of the meeting unnoticed.

19. (Sawbones / Queer Street / Juggernaut)-like, the bad news started to come in.

20. The angry workers (screwed / veined / distained) the truth out of their dishonest foreman.

UNIT II: SEARCH FOR MR HYDE

WORDS & MEANINGS ~ GROUP A

dry: dull

divinity: religious writer

endorsed: marked

holograph: handwritten

decease: death

benefactor: financial supporter

burthen: burden

eyesore: irritant

hitherto: previously

attributes: qualities

baffled: perturbed

presentment: appearance

fiend: devil

obnoxious: offensive

citadel: fortress

dapper: well-dressed

boisterous: lively

decided: determined

geniality: friendliness

reposed: was based

WHERE TO FIND THEM

The above words appear in the following section of 'Search For Mr Hyde':

From the START of the paragraph that begins with

That evening Mr Utterson came home to his bachelor house in sombre spirits and sat down to dinner without relish. It was his custom...

to the END of the paragraph that begins with

The solemn butler knew and welcomed him; he was subjected to no stage of delay, but ushered direct from the door to the dining-room...

BEFORE YOU START

Once you've reviewed the target words above, use this space to make a note of (i) all the words that you didn't know (before reading the meanings) and/or (ii) all the words you're uncertain about.

The words that you make a note of here are the words that you want to make sure that you've mastered by the time you get to the end of this part of the unit.

II.I For the following, match the word(s) in bold on the left to the correct definition in the numbered list. Write your answers on the given line.

dry	1. religious writer	_____
divinity	2. was based	_____
endorsed	3. fortress	_____
holograph	4. lively	_____
decease	5. burden	_____
benefactor	6. devil	_____
burthen	7. qualities	_____
eyesore	8. offensive	_____
hitherto	9. handwritten	_____
attributes	10. death	_____
baffled	11. perturbed	_____
presentment	12. marked	_____
fiend	13. determined	_____
obnoxious	14. friendliness	_____
citadel	15. well-dressed	_____
dapper	16. appearance	_____
boisterous	17. previously	_____
decided	18. dull	_____
geniality	19. financial supporter	_____
reposed	20. irritant	_____

1. **baffled**	clashed muted perturbed protruded
2. **dapper**	well informed well-acquainted well-fabricated well-dressed
3. **decided**	determined hesitated undirected eliminated
4. **attributes**	quantities quadrants questions qualities
5. **presentment**	appearance anticipation assurance aping
6. **benefactor**	financial supporter legal advocate religious disciple social worker
7. **divinity**	legal writer philosophical writer scientific writer religious writer
8. **holograph**	handwritten three-dimensional virtual printed
9. **hitherto**	therefore subsequently thenceforth previously
10. **obnoxious**	toxic enigmatic offensive paradoxical
11. **boisterous**	decorous lively coniferous frank
12. **burthen**	baggage cargo burden package
13. **eyesore**	defect irritant stye carbuncle
14. **reposed**	was based was sent was regarded was buried
15. **decease**	death worth hearth growth
16. **dry**	depressing discreet dull dangerous
17. **citadel**	stockade fortress mansion garrison
18. **geniality**	perceptiveness friendliness courtliness frivolousness
19. **endorsed**	enveloped unblemished corrected marked
20. **fiend**	scamp devil ally fairy

1. We were greatly (baffled / endorsed / reposed) by the suggestion that the thief was one of us.

2. With the (decease / divinity / geniality) of the rightful heir, the country descended into turmoil.

3. Entering the boardroom, the CEO wore a (dapper / deceased / decided) expression on her face.

4. This copy of the novel contains (eyesore / holograph / hitherto) emendations by the editor.

5. I'm afraid I found that wildlife documentary rather (dry / dapper / genial).

6. "Mr Collins is a man of admirable (fiends / citadels / attributes)!" enthused Mrs Bennet.

7. You'll find works by that Victorian (holograph / burthen / divinity) in the British Library.

8. The dukes' pact (reposed / attributes / burthened) upon their respect for each other.

9. Dr Faustus commanded the (holograph / fiend / burthen) to bring him unimaginable riches.

10. "Here, you can see where the writer (reposed / baffled / endorsed) her letter," said the scholar.

11. That pile of rubbish isn't just an (eyesore / attribute / holograph); it's unhygienic.

12. "I love my cousins, but they are rather (endorsed / boisterous / reposed)," confessed Rania.

13. The (Benefactor / Holograph / Citadel) of Saladin, in Cairo, was built in the twelfth century.

14. Admission to the club had (boisterously / hitherto / dapperly) been restricted.

15. The (divinity / citadel / geniality) of our welcome by the residents was a pleasant surprise.

16. The (hitherto / dapper / baffled) young man in the photograph sported a cheeky smile.

17. Cathy's sudden and wild (presentment / divinity / geniality) gave us all cause for alarm.

18. "Her comments are always shockingly (obnoxious / deceased / dapper)," Paulina noted.

19. The (decease / burthen / eyesore) of his guilt lay heavily upon the young shepherd.

20. The orphan's (benefactor / fiend / citadel) desired to remain anonymous.

UNIT II: SEARCH FOR MR HYDE

WORDS & MEANINGS ~ GROUP B

fanciful: irrational

balderdash: nonsense

estranged: alienated

Damon and Pythias: loyal friends

conveyancing: transferring ownership

composure: calmness

protégé: student

besieged: overwhelmed

dwelling: house

gross: total

bidding: commands

inordinate: excessive

bondage: enslavement

bowels of mercy: tenderness

concourse: crowdedness

quaint: odd

footfalls: footsteps

arrested: attracted

prevision: prediction

apropos: given this

WHERE TO FIND THEM

The above words appear in the following section of 'Search For Mr Hyde':

From the START of the paragraph that begins with

"We had," was the reply. "But it is more than ten years since Henry Jekyll became too fanciful for me. He began to go wrong...

to the START of the paragraph that begins with

"Yes," returned Mr Hyde, "It is as well we have met; and apropos, you should have my address." And he gave a number...

BEFORE YOU START

Once you've reviewed the target words above, use this space to make a note of (i) all the words that you didn't know (before reading the meanings) and/or (ii) all the words you're uncertain about.

The words that you make a note of here are the words that you want to make sure that you've mastered by the time you get to the end of this part of the unit.

II.4 Match the given words on the left to their correct meanings on the right. Then, use the letter to complete the definition statements below.

SMALL ANSWER: *Z is the meaning of **happy***

Words	Meanings
fanciful	A. total
balderdash	B. irrational
estranged	C. odd
Damon and Pythias	D. nonsense
conveyancing	E. transferring ownership
composure	F. student
protégé	G. attracted
besieged	H. excessive
dwelling	I. loyal friends
gross	J. overwhelmed
bidding	K. footsteps
inordinate	L. commands
bondage	M. enslavement
bowels of mercy	N. calmness
concourse	O. given this
quaint	P. tenderness
footfalls	Q. crowdedness
arrested	R. house
prevision	S. prediction
apropos	T. alienated

1. ___ is the meaning of **fanciful**.

2. ___ is the meaning of **balderdash**.

3. ___ is the meaning of **estranged**.

4. ___ is the meaning of **Damon and Pythias**.

5. ___ is the meaning of **conveyancing**.

6. ___ is the meaning of **composure**.

7. ___ is the meaning of **protégé**.

8. ___ is the meaning of **besieged**.

9. ___ is the meaning of **dwelling**.

10. ___ is the meaning of **gross**.

11. ___ is the meaning of **bidding**.

12. ___ is the meaning of **inordinate**.

13. ___ is the meaning of **bondage**.

14. ___ is the meaning of **bowels of mercy**.

15. ___ is the meaning of **concourse**.

16. ___ is the meaning of **quaint**.

17. ___ is the meaning of **footfalls**.

18. ___ is the meaning of **arrested**.

19. ___ is the meaning of **prevision**.

20. ___ is the meaning of **apropos**.

II.5 For this exercise, you'll need to refer to your copy of *Dr Jekyll & Mr Hyde.* First, turn to 'Search For Mr Hyde' and **find the paragraph that begins: 'This little spirit of temper...'.**

Once you've found the paragraph, start reading until you encounter each of the words in bold below. When you locate a word: **(a)** Write out the phrase, clause, or sentence in which it appears; and then **(b)** Rewrite the phrase, clause, or sentence and replace Stevenson's word with the meaning you've learnt. You may consult the text as often as you need to.

SAMPLE ANSWER:
*1. **feat***
*a. the **feat** was easy to Mr Utterson*
*b. the **endeavour** was easy to Mr Utterson*

1. **composure**

a. _____

b. _____

2. **protégé**

a. _____

b. _____

3. **besieged**

a. _____

b. _____

4. **dwelling**

a. _____

b. _____

5. **gross**

a. _____

b. _____

1. The industrialist's (balderdash / protégé / footfalls) rose to greater heights than her mentor.

2. Hearing (footfalls / balderdash / protégés) behind him, Sherlock Holmes whirled round.

3. Letitia's (dwelling / composure / concourse) in the face of such excitement irritated her sister.

4. We were (arrested / estranged / besieged) by grief when we heard the tragic news.

5. Cassandra's (conveyancing / prevision / concourse) of the fall of Troy was ignored by all.

6. Cruel and callous, the assassin was without (bondage / bowels of mercy / bidding).

7. Rudolph keeps a (quaint / gross / apropos) bronze statue on his desk.

8. The paperwork involved in (prevision / concourse / conveyancing) can be quite tiresome.

9. "My son and I have been much (gross / arrested / estranged) these past years," the earl said.

10. As a child, Laura's (apropos / fanciful / estranged) belief in ghosts was unshakeable.

11. "We shall live in (bowels of mercy / conveyancing / bondage) no longer!" roared the gladiators.

12. I've now received the letter, and (fancifully / quaintly / apropos), will review the matter.

13. "You will do my every (protégé / bidding / balderdash)," the sorcerer hissed.

14. The (footfalls / bidding / concourse) of the square was remarkable given the late hour.

15. The two girls were like (Damon and Pythias / bowels of mercy / protégés): forever constant.

16. There has been an (estranged / besieged / inordinate) amount of interest in this heist.

17. "This accusation is complete (conveyancing / apropos / balderdash)!" insisted Bernie.

18. The manager has been accused of (fanciful / arrested / gross) negligence.

19. The old cobbler's (concourse / dwelling / bondage) may have been humble, but it was his.

20. Felix's attention was (arrested / estranged / conveyed) by Leah's curious bracelet.

Unit II: Search For Mr Hyde

WORDS & MEANINGS ~ GROUP C

disquietude: uneasiness

perplexity: confusion

malformation: abnormality

timidity: lack of confidence

troglodytic: primitive

transpires: shines

transfigures: transforms

clay continent: human body

fanlight: window

flags: flagstones

cabinets: cupboards

wont: accustomed

dissecting room: anatomy theatre

statute of limitations: time limit

***pede claudo*:** on limping foot (i.e. delayed)

condoned: accepted

brooded: dwelled

iniquity: immoral behaviour

apprehension: anxiety

conceived: formed

WHERE TO FIND THEM

The above words appear in the following section of 'Search For Mr Hyde':

From the START of the paragraph that begins with

The lawyer stood awhile when Mr Hyde had left him, the picture of disquietude. Then he began slowly to...

to the END of the paragraph that begins with

And the lawyer set out homeward with a very heavy heart. "Poor Harry Jekyll," he thought, "my mind misgives me he is in deep waters! He was wild...

BEFORE YOU START

Once you've reviewed the target words above, use this space to make a note of (i) all the words that you didn't know (before reading the meanings) and/or (ii) all the words you're uncertain about.

The words that you make a note of here are the words that you want to make sure that you've mastered by the time you get to the end of this part of the unit.

II.7 Read the definition statements below and decide whether each is correct or incorrect. If the definition is correct, mark it with a capital 'T'. If it is incorrect, mark it with a capital 'F'.

1. The word **brooded** means **dwelled**. _____

2. The word **transfigures** means **primitive**. _____

3. The word **condoned** means **accepted**. _____

4. The words **dissecting room** mean **anatomy theatre**. _____

5. The word **malformation** means **uneasiness**. _____

6. The word **disquietude** means **window**. _____

7. The word **timidity** means **human body**. _____

8. The words **clay continent** mean **flagstones**. _____

9. The words *pede claudo* mean **on limping foot (i.e. delayed)**. _____

10. The word **flags** means **transforms**. _____

11. The words **statute of limitations** mean **time limit**. _____

12. The word **apprehension** means **anxiety**. _____

13. The word **wont** means **accustomed**. _____

14. The word **fanlight** means **lack of confidence**. _____

15. The word **perplexity** means **shines**. _____

16. The word **cabinets** means **cupboards**. _____

17. The word **transpires** means **confusion**. _____

18. The word **troglodytic** means **abnormality**. _____

19. The word **conceived** means **formed**. _____

20. The word **iniquity** means **immoral behaviour**. _____

II.8 Each of the following groups of words are antonyms for one of the target words in this section of the unit. Read each group carefully and then complete the statement using one of the words in the word bank below. Each word may be used only once.

SAMPLE ANSWER:
Z. miserable — morose — down — sad
The word <u>upbeat</u> is an antonym of all the above words.

WORD BANK

brooded   iniquity   malformation   perplexity

apprehension   troglodytic   timidity   condoned

A. sophisticated — civilized — cultivated — refined

The word _____ is an antonym of all the above words.

B. disregarded — ignored — discounted — dismissed

The word _____ is an antonym of all the above words.

C. denounced — condemned — censured — criticised

The word _____ is an antonym of all the above words.

D. virtue — decency — propriety — morality

The word _____ is an antonym of all the above words.

E. assurance — fearlessness — confidence — assertiveness

The word _____ is an antonym of all the above words.

F. calmness — serenity — tranquillity — peace

The word _____ is an antonym of all the above words.

G. regularity — usualness — normality — commonness

The word _____ is an antonym of all the above words.

H. enlightenment — clarity — lucidity — coherence

The word _____ is an antonym of all the above words.

1. The new students filed nervously into the (dissecting room / fanlight / statute of limitations).

2. The (malformations / fanlights / flags) in the courtyard were overgrown with weeds.

3. As was her (statute of limitations / *pede claudo* / wont), Julia went for a walk at 6 o'clock sharp.

4. The fact that he had been betrayed caused the king much (disquietude / *pede claudo* / timidity).

5. Juno has (brooded / conceived / transpired) a bad impression of her new neighbours.

6. "Try to overcome your (flag / timidity / clay continent)," the mouse advised the cowardly lion.

7. The phrase (clay continent / statute of limitations / dissecting room) is alliterative.

8. Sandy awaited his test results with considerable (apprehension / fanlight / malformation).

9. Eva stared at the nonsensical message in a state of (iniquity / malformation / perplexity).

10. Should there be a (wont / statute of limitations / perplexity) on serious crimes?

11. "Your actions will not be (brooded / conceived / condoned) if they're dishonest," Hugo warned.

12. The light that shone through the (cabinets / iniquities / fanlight) promised a warm welcome.

13. This new app completely (condones / perplexes / transfigures) our photo editing capabilities.

14. If you look in those (flags / clay continents / cabinets), you might find some spare linen.

15. Jacques sat and (condoned / brooded / transfigured) on how to resolve the problem.

16. Mark my words, your just desserts will follow (malformation / *pede claudo* / timidly).

17. "We will not tolerate such (iniquity / flags / *pede claudo*)," warned the patriarch.

18. Which (troglodytic / fanlight / transfigured) people produced these stunning cave paintings?

19. Her goodness (disquiets / transpires / flags) in everything that she does.

20. The (malformation / apprehension / transpiration) in the mummy was inexplicable.

Unit III: Dr Jekyll Was Quite At Ease

WORDS & MEANINGS

cronies: friends

contrived: arranged

loose-tongued: talkative

threshold: doorstep

unobtrusive: restrained

hide-bound: conservative

pedant: purist

blatant: unashamed

a trifle: a little

abominable: loathsome

incoherency of manner: hysteria

make a clean breast of: confess

downright: absolutely

irrepressible: uncontrollable

WHERE TO FIND THEM

The above words appear in the following section of 'Dr Jekyll Was Quite At Ease':

From the START of the paragraph that begins with

A fortnight later, by excellent good fortune, the doctor gave one of his pleasant dinners to some five or six old cronies, all intelligent, reputable men...

to the FINAL paragraph

Utterson heaved an irrepressible sigh. "Well," said he, "I promise."

BEFORE YOU START

Once you've reviewed the target words above, use this space to make a note of (i) all the words that you didn't know (before reading the meanings) and/or (ii) all the words you're uncertain about.

The words that you make a note of here are the words that you want to make sure that you've mastered by the time you get to the end of this unit.

1. a little
   a. a trifle   b. contrived   c. downright   d. irrepressible

2. doorstep
   a. a trifle   b. cronies   c. threshold   d. pedant

3. confess
   a. irrepressible   b. downright   c. blatant   d. make a clean breast of

4. talkative
   a. abominable   b. loose-tongued   c. irrepressible   d. contrived

5. restrained
   a. downright   b. unobtrusive   c. blatant   d. hide-bound

6. conservative
   a. hide-bound   b. abominable   c. unobtrusive   d. downright

7. friends
   a. thresholds   b. pedants   c. cronies   d. irrepressible

8. loathsome
   a. blatant   b. hide-bound   c. loose-tongued   d. abominable

9. unashamed
   a. loose-tongued   b. blatant   c. contrived   d. abominable

10. arranged
    a. contrived   b. downright   c. hide-bound   d. loose-tongued

11. purist
    a. pedant   b. incoherency of manner   c. downright   d. a trifle

12. absolutely
    a. make a clean breast of   b. unobtrusive   c. cronies   d. downright

13. hysteria
    a. contrived   b. incoherency of manner   c. downright   d. loose-tongued

14. uncontrollable
    a. incoherency of manner   b. make a clean breast of   c. irrepressible   d. blatant

III.2 For this exercise, you'll need to refer to your copy of *Dr Jekyll & Mr Hyde.* First, turn to 'Dr Jekyll Was Quite At Ease' and **find the paragraph that begins: 'What I heard was...'.**

Once you've found the paragraph, start reading until you encounter each of the words in bold below. When you locate a word: **(a)** Write out the phrase, clause, or sentence in which it appears; and then **(b)** Rewrite the phrase, clause, or sentence and replace Stevenson's word with the meaning you've learnt. You may consult the text as often as you need to.

Sample Answer:
1. *feat*
a. the *feat* was easy to Mr Utterson
b. the *endeavour* was easy to Mr Utterson

1. **abominable**

a. _____

b. _____

2. **incoherency of manner**

a. _____

b. _____

3. **make a clean breast of**

a. _____

b. _____

4. **downright**

a. _____

b. _____

5. **irrepressible**

a. _____

b. _____

1. *an excellent fellow [...] but a hide-bound <u>pedant</u> for all that*
   a. scientist   b. purist   c. friend   d. lawyer

2. *an ignorant, <u>blatant</u> pedant*
   a. unashamed   b. talkative   c. uncontrollable   d. loathsome

3. *I am a man to be trusted. <u>Make a clean breast of</u> this in confidence*
   a. entrust   b. conceal   c. announce   d. confess

4. *Mr Utterson so <u>contrived</u> that he remained behind after the others had departed*
   a. restrained   b. desired   c. arranged   d. confessed

5. *when the light-hearted and loose-tongued had already their foot on the <u>threshold</u>*
   a. gable   b. doorstep   c. eaves   d. door frame

6. *the doctor gave one of his pleasant dinners to some five or six old <u>cronies</u>*
   a. friends   b. rivals   c. conservatives   d. purists

7. *"You do not understand my position," returned the doctor, with [an] <u>incoherency of manner</u>*
   a. talkativeness   b. conservativism   c. hysteria   d. stubbornness

8. *when the light-hearted and <u>loose-tongued</u> had already their foot on the threshold*
   a. conservative   b. untruthful   c. restrained   d. talkative

9. *"What I heard was <u>abominable</u>," said Utterson*
   a. hysterical   b. loathsome   c. non-conservative   d. unrestrained

10. *that <u>hide-bound</u> pedant, Lanyon*
    a. conservative   b. loathsome   c. talkative   d. unashamed

11. *"My will? Yes, certainly, I know that," said the doctor, <u>a trifle</u> sharply*
    a. a little   b. a great deal   c. per usual   d. very much

12. *they liked to sit a while in his <u>unobtrusive</u> company, practising for solitude*
    a. uncontrollable   b. restrained   c. loathsome   d. talkative

13. *Utterson heaved an <u>irrepressible</u> sigh*
    a. unashamed   b. silent   c. uncontrollable   d. hysterical

UNIT IV: THE CAREW MURDER CASE

WORDS & MEANINGS ~ GROUP A

singular: exceptional

rendered: made

accosted: approached

trifling: playing

brandishing: waving

mangled: injured

insensate: senseless

whither: where

quailed: recoiled

stature: height

pall: dark cloud

routing: blowing away

hues: colours

lurid: intense

conflagration: fire

WHERE TO FIND THEM

The above words appear in the following section of 'The Carew Murder Case':

From the START of the paragraph that begins with

Nearly a year later, in the month of October, 18—, London was startled by a crime of singular ferocity and rendered all the more notable...

to the MIDDLE of the paragraph that begins with

It was by this time about nine in the morning, and the first fog of the season. A great chocolate-coloured pall lowered over heaven...

BEFORE YOU START

Once you've reviewed the target words above, use this space to make a note of (i) all the words that you didn't know (before reading the meanings) and/or (ii) all the words you're uncertain about.

The words that you make a note of here are the words that you want to make sure that you've mastered by the time you get to the end of this part of the unit.

IV.I Match the given words on the left to their correct meanings on the right. Then, use the letter to complete the definition statements below.

SAMPLE ANSWER: _Z_ is the meaning of **happy**

Words	Meanings
singular	A. waving
rendered	B. intense
accosted	C. colours
trifling	D. dark cloud
brandishing	E. senseless
mangled	F. playing
insensate	G. exceptional
whither	H. injured
quailed	I. approached
stature	J. height
pall	K. fire
routing	L. blowing away
hues	M. where
lurid	N. recoiled
conflagration	O. made

1. ___ is the meaning of **singular**.

2. ___ is the meaning of **rendered**.

3. ___ is the meaning of **accosted**.

4. ___ is the meaning of **trifling**.

5. ___ is the meaning of **brandishing**.

6. ___ is the meaning of **mangled**.

7. ___ is the meaning of **insensate**.

8. ___ is the meaning of **whither**.

9. ___ is the meaning of **quailed**.

10. ___ is the meaning of **stature**.

11. ___ is the meaning of **pall**.

12. ___ is the meaning of **routing**.

13. ___ is the meaning of **hues**.

14. ___ is the meaning of **lurid**.

15. ___ is the meaning of **conflagration**.

1. **conflagration**   fire   standard   group   battle

2. **trifling**   polishing   playing   pointing   prodding

3. **brandishing**   igniting   stamping   guarding   waving

4. **routing**   drawing towards   blowing away   pushing against   running into

5. **insensate**   senseless   sensible   sensational   incensed

6. **lurid**   ridiculous   hollow   intense   elaborate

7. **pall**   dark room   dark thought   dark liquid   dark cloud

8. **singular**   normal   exceptional   casual   liberal

9. **hues**   cries   colours   complications   canvases

10. **rendered**   torn   misrepresented   withheld   made

11. **stature**   height   weight   width   depth

12. **mangled**   inflated   inebriated   injured   intruded

13. **whither**   wilt   forth   where   thence

14. **quailed**   argued   recoiled   exclaimed   recovered

15. **accosted**   approached   admonished   appraised   attacked

IV.3 For the following, choose the one option from those listed that reflects the most correct meaning of the underlined word(s) as used by Stevenson in each of the given extracts below.

1. *the older man bowed and <u>accosted</u> the other with a very pretty manner of politeness*
   a. insulted   b. approached   c. injured   d. departed

2. *the wind was continually charging and <u>routing</u> these embattled vapours*
   a. moving towards   b. blowing away   c. playing with   d. waving at

3. *London was startled by a crime of <u>singular</u> ferocity*
   a. senseless   b. exceptional   c. common   d. expected

4. *Mr Utterson had already <u>quailed</u> at the name of Hyde*
   a. recoiled   b. frowned   c. approached   d. smiled

5. *there would be a glow of a rich, <u>lurid</u> brown*
   a. familiar   b. opaque   c. disgusting   d. intense

6. *<u>rendered</u> all the more notable by the high position of the victim*
   a. remembered   b. narrated   c. made   d. reported

7. *A great chocolate-coloured <u>pall</u> lowered over heaven*
   a. dark flag   b. dark curtain   c. dark cloud   d. dark sheet

8. *there lay his victim in the middle of the lane, incredibly <u>mangled</u>*
   a. motionless   b. injured   c. distressed   d. silent

9. *The stick [...] had broken in the middle under the stress of this <u>insensate</u> cruelty*
   a. exceptional   b. fiery   c. dark   d. senseless

10. *He had in his hand a heavy cane, with which he was <u>trifling</u>*
    a. playing   b. leaning   c. shaking   d. walking

11. *stamping with his foot, <u>brandishing</u> the cane, and carrying on [...] like a madman*
    a. waving   b. rolling   c. tapping   d. thudding

12. *"Is this Mr Hyde a person of small <u>stature</u>?" he inquired*
    a. intelligence   b. weight   c. reputation   d. height

13. *like the light of some strange <u>conflagration</u>*
    a. dark cloud   b. star   c. candle   d. fire

UNIT IV: THE CAREW MURDER CASE

WORDS & MEANINGS ~ GROUP B

slatternly: scruffy

kindled: lit

assail: attack

gin palace: pub

umber: dark (brown) pigment

blackguardly: disreputable

hypocrisy: insincerity

odious: unpleasant

napery: household linen

connoisseur: expert judge

ransacked: searched

hearth: fireplace

disinterred: unearthed

familiars: friends

fugitive: runaway

WHERE TO FIND THEM

The above words appear in the following section of 'The Carew Murder Case':

From the MIDDLE of the paragraph that begins with

It was by this time about nine in the morning, and the first fog of the season. A great chocolate-coloured pall lowered over heaven...

to the END of the paragraph that begins with

This last, however, was not so easy of accomplishment; for Mr Hyde had numbered few familiars—even the master of the servant maid had only seen him twice...

BEFORE YOU START

Once you've reviewed the target words above, use this space to make a note of (i) all the words that you didn't know (before reading the meanings) and/or (ii) all the words you're uncertain about.

The words that you make a note of here are the words that you want to make sure that you've mastered by the time you get to the end of this part of the unit.

IV.4 For the following, match the word(s) in bold on the left to the correct definition in the numbered list. Write your answers on the given line.

slatternly	1. unearthed	_____
kindled	2. searched	_____
assail	3. expert judge	_____
gin palace	4. pub	_____
umber	5. unpleasant	_____
blackguardly	6. insincerity	_____
hypocrisy	7. lit	_____
odious	8. runaway	_____
napery	9. friends	_____
connoisseur	10. fireplace	_____
ransacked	11. attack	_____
hearth	12. household linen	_____
disinterred	13. scruffy	_____
familiars	14. disreputable	_____
fugitive	15. dark (brown) pigment	_____

IV.5 Build a Word Web of your associations with each of the words supplied in the following diagrams. The labels in each of the boxes have been provided to help guide your thoughts. Add more links and boxes of your own if you think of them!

SAMPLE ANSWER:

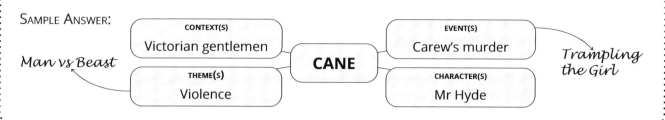

Man vs Beast

| CONTEXT(S) Victorian gentlemen | CANE | EVENT(S) Carew's murder | Trampling the Girl |

THEME(S) Violence — CHARACTER(S) Mr Hyde

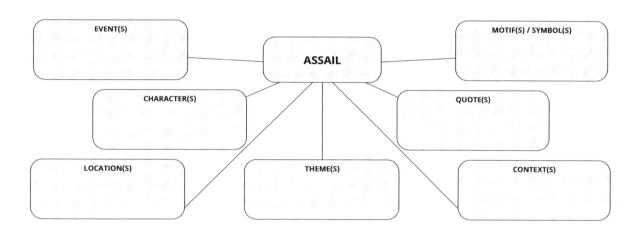

ASSAIL

- EVENT(S)
- MOTIF(S) / SYMBOL(S)
- CHARACTER(S)
- QUOTE(S)
- LOCATION(S)
- THEME(S)
- CONTEXT(S)

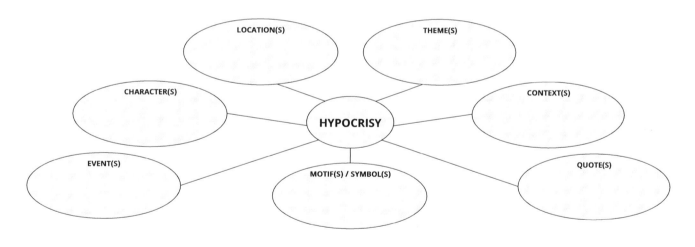

HYPOCRISY

- LOCATION(S)
- THEME(S)
- CHARACTER(S)
- CONTEXT(S)
- EVENT(S)
- MOTIF(S) / SYMBOL(S)
- QUOTE(S)

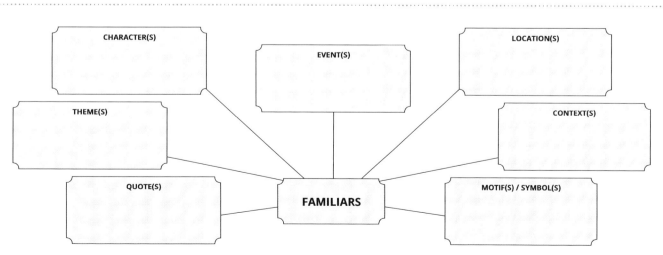

FAMILIARS

- CHARACTER(S)
- EVENT(S)
- LOCATION(S)
- THEME(S)
- CONTEXT(S)
- QUOTE(S)
- MOTIF(S) / SYMBOL(S)

1. *A flash of <u>odious</u> joy appeared upon the woman's face*
   a. scruffy   b. unearthly   c. searching   d. unpleasant

2. *on the <u>hearth</u> there lay a pile of grey ashes*
   a. household linen   b. curtains   c. cupboards   d. fireplace

3. *the haunting sense of unexpressed deformity with which the <u>fugitive</u> impressed his beholders*
   a. friend   b. runaway   c. servant   d. expert judge

4. *Mr Hyde had numbered few <u>familiars</u>*
   a. family members   b. servants   c. dependants   d. friends

5. *Henry Jekyll, who was much of a <u>connoisseur</u>*
   a. friend   b. runaway   c. expert judge   d. amateur

6. *its lamps, which had never been extinguished or had been <u>kindled</u> afresh*
   a. installed   b. oiled   c. lit   d. extinguished

7. *that terror of the law and the law's officers, which may at times <u>assail</u> the most honest*
   a. inform   b. attack   c. please   d. judge

8. *the rooms bore every mark of having been recently and hurriedly <u>ransacked</u>*
   a. searched   b. lit   c. unearthed   d. attacked

9. *the inspector <u>disinterred</u> the butt end of a green cheque book*
   a. attacked   b. searched   c. unearthed   d. lit

10. *the fog settled down again upon that part, as brown as <u>umber</u>*
    a. dark (brown) pigment   b. dark (brown) gemstone   c. dark (brown) earth   d. dark (brown) wood

11. *and cut him off from his <u>blackguardly</u> surroundings*
    a. unearthly   b. disreputable   c. fiery   d. friendless

12. *The dismal quarter of Soho [...] with its muddy ways, and <u>slatternly</u> passengers*
    a. fugitive   b. violent   c. scruffy   d. friendless

13. *the plate was of silver, the <u>napery</u> elegant; a good picture hung upon the walls*
    a. fireplace   b. household linen   c. curtains   d. cabinets

Unit V: Incident Of The Letter

anatomical: relating to the body

quarters: accommodation

gaunt: empty

cupola: domed skylight

baize: woollen cloth

cabinet: small private room

presses: cupboards

cheval glass: upright tilting mirror

ruminated: thought

signified: stated

qualm: fit

circulars: advertisements

oration: speech

eddy: whirlpool

ticklish: difficult

carbuncles: red gems

imperial: reddish-purple

counsel: the law

elicited: generated

sedulously: meticulously

WHERE TO FIND THEM

The above words appear in the following section of 'Incident Of The Letter':

From the START of the paragraph that begins with

It was late in the afternoon, when Mr Utterson found his way to Dr Jekyll's door, where he was at once admitted by Poole, and carried down by the kitchen offices...

to the START of the paragraph that begins with

"One moment. I thank you, sir;" and the clerk laid the two sheets of paper alongside and sedulously compared their contents. "Thank you, sir," he said...

BEFORE YOU START

Once you've reviewed the target words above, use this space to make a note of (i) all the words that you didn't know (before reading the meanings) and/or (ii) all the words you're uncertain about.

The words that you make a note of here are the words that you want to make sure that you've mastered by the time you get to the end of this unit.

1. The word **ruminated** means **generated**. _____

2. The words **cheval glass** mean **upright tilting mirror**.

3. The word **gaunt** means **empty**. _____

4. The word **qualm** means **meticulously**. _____

5. The word **anatomical** means **relating to the body**. _____

6. The word **carbuncles** means **advertisements**. _____

7. The word **quarters** means **accommodation**. _____

8. The word **elicited** means **thought**. _____

9. The word **ticklish** means **speech**. _____

10. The word **cabinet** means **small private room**. _____

11. The word **eddy** means **stated**. _____

12. The word **signified** means **difficult**. _____

13. The word **imperial** means **the law**. _____

14. The word **sedulously** means **reddish-purple**. _____

15. The word **counsel** means **red gems**. _____

16. The word **baize** means **woollen cloth**. _____

17. The word **cupola** means **domed skylight**. _____

18. The word **oration** means **fit**. _____

19. The word **circulars** means **whirlpool**. _____

20. The word **presses** means **cupboards**. _____

> V.2 For each of the following, select the one option from the choices on the right that is the correct synonym for the given word(s) in bold on the left.

1. **qualm**   calm   health   fit   dream

2. **quarters**   division   apparatus   beats   accommodation

3. **elicited**   generated   overlooked   ignored   exposed

4. **carbuncles**   blue gems   green gems   yellow gems   red gems

5. **oration**   idea   blessing   measurement   speech

6. **cabinet**   large cellar   tiny attic   outdoor public privy   small private room

7. **baize**   oil paint   thick paper   woollen cloth   antique wood

8. **ruminated**   rejoiced   thought   prayed   chuckled

9. **counsel**   the law   the police   the government   the clergy

10. **cheval glass** tumbler   upright tilting mirror   graduated cylinder   test tube

11. **presses**   cupboards   drawers   shelves   benches

12. **sedulously**   superficially   partially   meticulously   effortlessly

13. **imperial**   blueish-green   orange-yellow   reddish-purple   pearl white

14. **anatomical**   relating to the atom   relating to the body   relating to physics   relating to chemistry

15. **signified**   omitted   stated   quietened   ignored

16. **ticklish**   confusing   uncomplicated   enraging   difficult

17. **circulars**   bills   advertisements   paperbacks   magazines

18. **cupola**   fanlight   rose window   gable   domed skylight

19. **eddy**   stream   drain   whirlpool   sewer

20. **gaunt**   empty   aged   overflowing   bright

1. In this medieval text, (carbuncles / qualms / counsels) are attributed with magical properties.

2. Having (ruminated / signified / eddied) for several days, Omar finally reached a decision.

3. Kristen's announcement (signified / tickled / elicited) no response from her aunt.

4. Desiring some peace and quiet, Mr Bennet retreated to his (cabinet / presses / circulars) to read.

5. Brunelleschi's Dome is perhaps the most famous (cupola / cheval glass / eddy) of all.

6. The mayor has (elicited / signified / eddied) that she is willing to meet us.

7. We receive an annoyingly high number of (circulars / eddies / quarters) in our post.

8. At the end of the day, the servants retired gratefully to their (carbuncles / quarters / cupolas).

9. Lady Montgomery stood before her (cheval glass / cupola / baize) to admire her evening gown.

10. The (circulars / presses / counsels) in the alchemist's study were full of strange apparatus.

11. "(Carbuncles / Counsel / Cheval glass) is clear; you have no recourse," stated the lawyer.

12. In the forum, the Roman senator delivered an impassioned (carbuncle / oration / cupola).

13. After the guests' departure, Ophelia wandered through the (gaunt / sedulous / ticklish) ballroom.

14. The morning of his triumph, the Roman general donned his (signified / imperial / gaunt) toga.

15. "Don't put that on the billiard table; it'll ruin the (qualms / baize / cupola)!" I yelled.

16. Misreading his bank statement, Felix had a temporary (quarter / qualm / oration) of panic.

17. The (baize / elicit / anatomical) structure of this species enables it to fly faster than other birds.

18. One of my cats used to love watching the small (presses / baize / eddy) as the bath emptied.

19. "To be sure, 'twill be (elicited / anatomical / ticklish) to resolve this," observed Mrs Allen.

20. Wilma spent hours (gauntly / quarterly / sedulously) marking her students' essays.

UNIT VI: INCIDENT OF DR LANYON

resented: regarded negatively

ken: knowledge

unearthed: uncovered

disreputable: scandalous

callous: cold-hearted

blotted out: erased

seclusion: isolation

death warrant: death sentence

accursed: damned

drift: meaning

suffer: allow

amities: friendships

tenor: direction

trustee: executor

stringent: strict

disquieted: uneasy

bondage: imprisonment

inscrutable: enigmatic

recluse: hermit

fell off: decreased

WHERE TO FIND THEM

The above words appear in the following section of 'Incident Of Dr Lanyon':

From the START of the paragraph that begins with

Time ran on; thousands of pounds were offered in reward, for the death of Sir Danvers was resented as a public injury; but Mr Hyde had disappeared...

to the END of the paragraph that begins with

It is one thing to mortify curiosity, another to conquer it; and it may be doubted if, from that day forth, Utterson desired the society of his surviving friend...

BEFORE YOU START

Once you've reviewed the target words above, use this space to make a note of (i) all the words that you didn't know (before reading the meanings) and/or (ii) all the words you're uncertain about.

The words that you make a note of here are the words that you want to make sure that you've mastered by the time you get to the end of this unit.

VI.I For the following, match the word(s) in bold on the left to the correct definition in the numbered list. Write your answers on the given line.

Word		Definition
resented		1. direction
ken		2. strict
unearthed		3. damned
disreputable		4. erased
callous		5. knowledge
blotted out		6. regarded negatively
seclusion		7. cold-hearted
death warrant		8. uneasy
accursed		9. enigmatic
drift		10. allow
suffer		11. imprisonment
amities		12. hermit
tenor		13. isolation
trustee		14. decreased
stringent		15. meaning
disquieted		16. friendships
bondage		17. uncovered
inscrutable		18. death sentence
recluse		19. scandalous
fell off		20. executor

1. I find the Mona Lisa's (inscrutable / disreputable / blotted out) expression fascinating.

2. Hermione was clearly (unearthed / disquieted / accursed) as she waited for news.

3. For years, any knights captured on the evil lord's land were kept in (amities / bondage / tenor).

4. "I'll help you if you help me — if you get my (amity / ken / drift)," said Tomas slyly.

5. Jason's neighbour is something of a (recluse / tenor / drift); he hasn't seen her for over a year.

6. Oscar's mind has (blotted out / drifted / disquieted) the events of that terrible evening.

7. I am at my most efficient when I work in (tenor / recluse / seclusion).

8. The archaeological team have (resented / unearthed / accursed) some stunning artefacts.

9. Lord Montgomery would not (suffer / tenor / resent) his only son to join the army.

10. The admissions policies of that golf club are unusually (secluded / blotted out / stringent).

11. Harold (drifted / resented / disquieted) the affection that was lavished on his younger sister.

12. I am not comfortable with the (bondage / tenor / disrepute) her arguments are taking.

13. Aditi has been named a (trustee / recluse / tenor) of her grandfather's estate.

14. "Oh, (accursed / inscrutable / unearthed) day!" wailed Jasmine. "I've lost everything!"

15. Over the years, (tenors / amities / trustees) have grown between the families in our area.

16. "How (inscrutable / disquieted / callous) of you to embarrass Hattie like that!" scolded Regina.

17. The number of visitors to the village (unearthed / resented / fell off) markedly after the flood.

18. "His (disreputable / stringent / blotted out) elopement is unforgivable," stated Lady Essex flatly.

19. "How to lift this curse is beyond my (ken / seclusion / drift)," the witch admitted.

20. It was the vizier's murder of the princess that sealed his (ken / trustees / death warrant).

WORD BANK

inscrutable   resented   callous   accursed

disquieted   stringent   suffer   disreputable

A. calm — serene — tranquil — undisturbed

The word _____ is an antonym of all the above words.

B. imprecise — inexact — careless — unconscientious

The word _____ is an antonym of all the above words.

C. blessed — hallowed — divine — sanctified

The word _____ is an antonym of all the above words.

D. forbid — prevent — obstruct — bar

The word _____ is an antonym of all the above words.

E. welcomed — embraced — greeted — supported

The word _____ is an antonym of all the above words.

F. straightforward — candid — direct — unambiguous

The word _____ is an antonym of all the above words.

G. seemly — proper — decorous — honourable

The word _____ is an antonym of all the above words.

H. compassionate — pitying — humane — benevolent

The word _____ is an antonym of all the above words.

UNIT VII: INCIDENT AT THE WINDOW

WORDS & MEANINGS

repulsion: disgust

presence: company

premature: early

mien: expression

disconsolate: miserable

drearily: bleakly

whipping up: stimulating

circulation: blood flow

venture: dare

abject: stark

traversed: crossed

stirrings: movements

WHERE TO FIND THEM

The above words appear in the following section of 'Incident At The Window':

From the START of the paragraph that begins with

"I hope not," said Utterson. "Did I ever tell you that I once saw him, and shared your feeling of repulsion?"...

to the END of the paragraph that begins with

"That is just what I was about to venture to propose," returned the doctor with a smile. But the words were hardly uttered...

BEFORE YOU START

Once you've reviewed the target words above, use this space to make a note of (i) all the words that you didn't know (before reading the meanings) and/or (ii) all the words you're uncertain about.

The words that you make a note of here are the words that you want to make sure that you've mastered by the time you get to the end of this unit.

1. movements
    a. repulsion   b. disconsolate   c. stirrings   d. venture

2. blood flow
    a. whipping up   b. circulation   c. mien   d. stirrings

3. company
    a. venture   b. circulation   c. presence   d. repulsion

4. expression
    a. circulation   b. mien   c. venture   d. repulsion

5. disgust
    a. repulsion   b. mien   c. presence   d. premature

6. stimulating
    a. whipping up   b. stirrings   c. traversed   d. venture

7. early
    a. whipping up   b. stirrings   c. drearily   d. premature

8. bleakly
    a. drearily   b. premature   c. stirrings   d. traversed

9. dare
    a. presence   b. stirrings   c. venture   d. repulsion

10. stark
    a. traversed   b. premature   c. whipping up   d. abject

11. crossed
    a. disconsolate   b. venture   c. circulation   d. traversed

12. miserable
    a. presence   b. disconsolate   c. repulsion   d. mien

VII.2 For this exercise, you'll need to refer to your copy of *Dr Jekyll & Mr Hyde.* First, turn to 'Incident At The Window' and **find the paragraph that begins: "'I hope not...'**.

Once you've found the paragraph, start reading until you encounter each of the words in bold below. When you locate a word: **(a)** Write out the phrase, clause, or sentence in which it appears; and then **(b)** Rewrite the phrase, clause, or sentence and replace Stevenson's word with the meaning you've learnt. You may consult the text as often as you need to.

SAMPLE ANSWER:
1. feat
a. the feat was easy to Mr Utterson
b. the endeavour was easy to Mr Utterson

1. **repulsion**

a. _____

b. _____

2. **presence**

a. _____

b. _____

3. **premature**

a. _____

b. _____

4. **mien**

a. _____

b. _____

5. **disconsolate**

a. _____

b. _____

1. *"That is just what I was about to <u>venture</u> to propose," returned the doctor*
   a. insist   b. repeat   c. refuse   d. dare

2. *taking the air with an infinite sadness of <u>mien</u>*
   a. thought   b. movement   c. feeling   d. expression

3. *"You should be out, <u>whipping up</u> the circulation like Mr Enfield and me [...]"*
   a. punishing   b. stimulating   c. calming   d. checking

4. *"Did I ever tell you that I once saw him, and shared your feeling of <u>repulsion</u>?"*
   a. misery   b. bleakness   c. stimulation   d. disgust

5. *I feel as if the <u>presence</u> of a friend might do him good*
   a. loyalty   b. expression   c. company   d. movements

6. *"You should be out, whipping up the <u>circulation</u> like Mr Enfield and me [...]"*
   a. brain   b. blood flow   c. exercise   d. boredom

7. *The court was very cool and a little damp, and full of <u>premature</u> twilight*
   a. bleak   b. stark   c. early   d. miserable

8. *an expression of such <u>abject</u> terror and despair*
   a. stark   b. disgusting   c. motionless   d. expressionless

9. *even upon a Sunday there were still some <u>stirrings</u> of life*
   a. movements   b. absence   c. interference   d. contradictions

10. *In silence, too, they <u>traversed</u> the by-street*
    a. crossed   b. followed   c. noticed   d. avoided

11. *like some <u>disconsolate</u> prisoner*
    a. miserable   b. disgusted   c. daring   d. stimulated

12. *"I am very low, Utterson," replied the doctor <u>drearily</u>*
    a. angrily   b. repeatedly   c. irritably   d. bleakly

Unit VIII: The Last Night

Words & Meanings ~ Group A

doggedly: determinedly
foul play: criminal violence
wrack: cloud
diaphanous: fine
lawny: soft
peevishly: irritably
unseemly: improper
lamentation: weeping

get this through hands: deal with this
termination: concluding statement
lumber: jumble
resolution: will power
made away with: murdered
induce: persuade
hold water: make sense

Where to Find Them

The above words appear in the following section of 'The Last Night':

From the START of the paragraph that begins with

"I've been afraid for about a week," returned Poole, doggedly disregarding the question, "and I can bear it no more."...

to the END of the paragraph that begins with

"This is a very strange tale, Poole; this is rather a wild tale my man," said Mr Utterson, biting his finger...

Before You Start

Once you've reviewed the target words above, use this space to make a note of (i) all the words that you didn't know (before reading the meanings) and/or (ii) all the words you're uncertain about.

The words that you make a note of here are the words that you want to make sure that you've mastered by the time you get to the end of this part of the unit.

VIII.I Match the given words on the left to their correct meanings on the right. Then, use the letter to complete the definition statements below.

SAMPLE ANSWER: *Z is the meaning of **happy***

Words	Meanings
doggedly	A. make sense
foul play	B. deal with this
wrack	C. determinedly
diaphanous	D. persuade
lawny	E. fine
peevishly	F. will power
unseemly	G. jumble
lamentation	H. murdered
get this through hands	I. soft
termination	J. irritably
lumber	K. weeping
resolution	L. improper
made away with	M. cloud
induce	N. concluding statement
hold water	O. criminal violence

1. ___ is the meaning of **doggedly**.

2. ___ is the meaning of **foul play**.

3. ___ is the meaning of **wrack**.

4. ___ is the meaning of **diaphanous**.

5. ___ is the meaning of **lawny**.

6. ___ is the meaning of **peevishly**.

7. ___ is the meaning of **unseemly**.

8. ___ is the meaning of **lamentation**.

9. ___ is the meaning of **get this through hands**.

10. ___ is the meaning of **termination**.

11. ___ is the meaning of **lumber**.

12. ___ is the meaning of **resolution**.

13. ___ is the meaning of **made away with**.

14. ___ is the meaning of **induce**.

15. ___ is the meaning of **hold water**.

doggedly	**peevishly**	**lumber**
foul play	**unseemly**	**resolution**
wrack	**lamentation**	**made away with**
diaphanous	**get this through hands**	**induce**
lawny	**termination**	**hold water**

1. "By way of _____, I wish to share our vision of the future," the speaker announced.

2. "Don't interrupt me," said Sita _____. "I'm trying to concentrate."

3. High in the sky, the moon was gradually obscured by a large, slow-moving _____.

4. Upon seeing the body, Sherlock Holmes declared that _____ had been at work.

5. The attic was filled to the rafters with _____: old furniture and packing cases.

6. The _____ texture of the fabric was pleasing to the touch.

7. "Can I _____ you to join me for an after-supper stroll?" Mr Darcy inquired.

8. "It is _____ for a young woman to go about unchaperoned," sniffed Lady De Vere.

9. "When it comes to chocolate, all my _____ flies out of the window," confessed Mira.

10. "Don't despair; we'll _____," Molly's brother comforted her.

11. The bride's veil was a _____ affair that trailed more than two metres behind her.

12. As the news spread, the sound of women's _____ rose and filled the air.

13. The police believe the victim was _____ after she surprised the intruder.

14. "I don't buy your story; it doesn't _____," the journalist stated.

15. Sydney worked _____ to impress his new boss.

1. **unseemly**	improper untidy invisible frayed
2. **get this through hands**	pay for this deal with this regret this redo this
3. **lumber**	jamboree jim-jams jamb jumble
4. **resolution**	horse power water power powerhouse will power
5. **lawny**	coarse powdered soft grainy
6. **peevishly**	irritably patiently affably mischievously
7. **foul play**	making filthy unsportsmanlike behaviour criminal violence air pollution
8. **termination**	lengthy statement concluding statement ambiguous statement opening statement
9. **hold water**	make way make sense make sure make right
10. **lamentation**	covering repeating weeping ripping
11. **made away with**	confiscated discarded murdered fabricated
12. **doggedly**	tiredly hardly slavishly determinedly
13. **diaphanous**	opaque fine brittle rough
14. **wrack**	swarm crowd dimness cloud
15. **induce**	persuade refute whittle discourage

UNIT VIII: THE LAST NIGHT

WORDS & MEANINGS ~ GROUP B

maladies: illnesses

exorbitant: unreasonable

mottled: blotchy

pallor: paleness

poker: fire iron

vengeance: revenge

malefactor: criminal

scud: clouds

contorted: twisted

semblance: appearance

phial: small glass bottle

kernels: seeds

pious: devout

blasphemies: irreligious statements

penetration: discernment

WHERE TO FIND THEM

The above words appear in the following section of 'The Last Night':

From the START of the paragraph that begins with

"These are all very strange circumstances," said Mr Utterson, "but I think I begin to see daylight...

to the START of the paragraph that begins with

"My dear Utterson,—When this shall fall into your hands, I shall have disappeared, under what circumstances I have not the penetration to foresee...

BEFORE YOU START

Once you've reviewed the target words above, use this space to make a note of (i) all the words that you didn't know (before reading the meanings) and/or (ii) all the words you're uncertain about.

The words that you make a note of here are the words that you want to make sure that you've mastered by the time you get to the end of this part of the unit.

VIII.4 For the following, match the word(s) in bold on the left to the correct definition in the numbered list. Write your answers on the given line.

Word		Definition	
maladies		1. criminal	_____
exorbitant		2. clouds	_____
mottled		3. devout	_____
pallor		4. seeds	_____
poker		5. revenge	_____
vengeance		6. unreasonable	_____
malefactor		7. twisted	_____
scud		8. discernment	_____
contorted		9. fire iron	_____
semblance		10. paleness	_____
phial		11. irreligious statements	_____
kernels		12. small glass bottle	_____
pious		13. illnesses	_____
blasphemies		14. appearance	_____
penetration		15. blotchy	_____

VIII.5 Build a Word Web of your associations with each of the words supplied in the following diagrams. The labels in each of the boxes have been provided to help guide your thoughts. Add more links and boxes of your own if you think of them!

SAMPLE ANSWER:

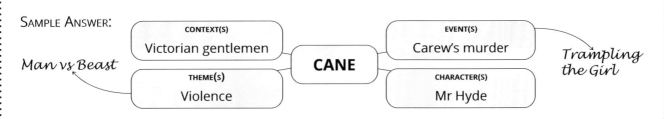

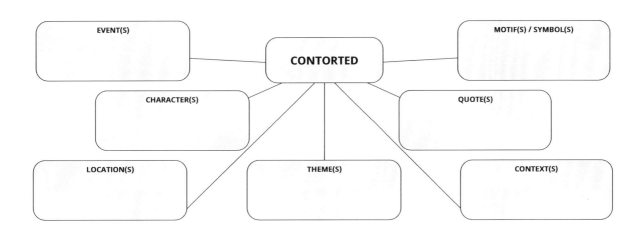

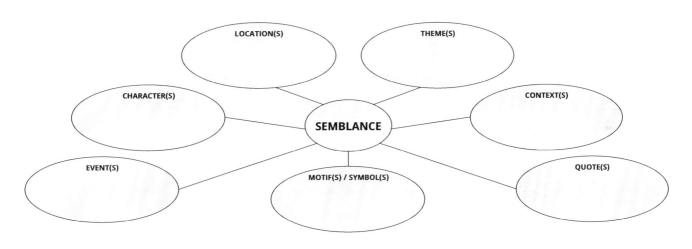

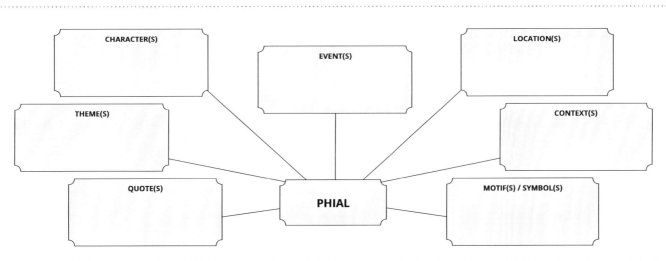

1. *you might take the kitchen <u>poker</u> for yourself*
    a. small glass bottle   b. bellows   c. fire iron   d. clothes press

2. *the crushed <u>phial</u> in the hand*
    a. fire iron   b. powder   c. small glass bottle   d. letter

3. *the cords of his face still moved with a <u>semblance</u> of life*
    a. paleness   b. redness   c. appearance   d. absence

4. *lest [...] any <u>malefactor</u> seek to escape by the back*
    a. visitor   b. criminal   c. devotee   d. divinity

5. *The <u>scud</u> had banked over the moon*
    a. eclipse   b. lightning   c. thunder   d. clouds

6. *one of those <u>maladies</u> that both torture and deform the sufferer*
    a. criminals   b. illnesses   c. clouds   d. fire irons

7. *under what circumstances I have not the <u>penetration</u> to foresee*
    a. piety   b. discernment   c. health   d. strength

8. *it is plain and natural, hangs well together, and delivers us from all <u>exorbitant</u> alarms*
    a. unreasonable   b. vengeful   c. apparent   d. irreligious

9. *Utterson was amazed to find it a copy of a <u>pious</u> work*
    a. devout   b. irreligious   c. criminal   d. vengeful

10. *the butler, turning to a sort of <u>mottled</u> pallor*
    a. pale   b. unreasonable   c. sick   d. blotchy

11. *the butler, turning to a sort of mottled <u>pallor</u>*
    a. cloudiness   b. redness   c. paleness   d. greyness

12. *let our name be <u>vengeance</u>*
    a. revenge   b. devotion   c. friendship   d. anger

13. *annotated, in his own hand with startling <u>blasphemies</u>*
    a. irreligious statements   b. prayers   c. poems   d. formula

Unit IX: Dr Lanyon's Narrative

Words & Meanings ~ Group A

intercourse: conversation

morbid: dreadful

capital: utmost

farrago: confusion

hansom: a horse-drawn carriage used as a taxi

pungent: strong-smelling

appended: added

whetted: triggered

flighty: unstable

impediment: obstacle

posture: state

constrained: restricted

constitution: physical strength

incipient rigour: goose pimples

idiosyncratic: peculiar

Where to Find Them

The above words appear in the following section of 'Dr Lanyon's Narrative':

From the START of the paragraph that begins with

On the ninth of January, now four days ago, I received by the evening delivery a registered envelope...

to the END of the paragraph that begins with

These particulars struck me, I confess, disagreeably; and as I followed him into the bright light of the consulting room...

Before You Start

Once you've reviewed the target words above, use this space to make a note of (i) all the words that you didn't know (before reading the meanings) and/or (ii) all the words you're uncertain about.

The words that you make a note of here are the words that you want to make sure that you've mastered by the time you get to the end of this part of the unit.

IX.I For the following, match the word(s) in bold on the left to the correct definition in the numbered list. Write your answers on the given line.

intercourse	1. added	_____
morbid	2. peculiar	_____
capital	3. state	_____
farrago	4. confusion	_____
hansom	5. unstable	_____
pungent	6. physical strength	_____
appended	7. restricted	_____
whetted	8. strong-smelling	_____
flighty	9. dreadful	_____
impediment	10. triggered	_____
posture	11. a horse-drawn carriage used as a taxi	_____
constrained	12. obstacle	_____
constitution	13. conversation	_____
incipient rigour	14. goose pimples	_____
idiosyncratic	15. utmost	_____

intercourse	pungent	posture
morbid	appended	constrained
capital	whetted	constitution
farrago	flighty	incipient rigour
hansom	impediment	idiosyncratic

1. "My good man, would you hail me a _____?" the top-hatted gentleman inquired.

2. "Regular walks are necessary to maintain one's _____," Mr Garland urged.

3. Black Friday sales are invariably accompanied by scenes of widespread _____.

4. A lack of funds has _____ the company's expansion plans.

5. We've been told there is no legal _____ to our planned course of action.

6. Discovering his uncle's betrayal _____ Hamlet's desire for revenge.

7. One _____ aspect of pangolins is that, although mammals, they are covered in scales.

8. When one is cold, one may well experience _____.

9. "Identifying the victim is of _____ importance," announced Inspector Lestrade.

10. The company has striven to retain its competitive _____ in the market.

11. "I've _____ my notes to the end of your essay," Professor Hassan told me.

12. "How CAN you eat that _____ cheese?!" Amira asked in disbelief.

13. All the _____ yesterday was dominated by discussions of current political events.

14. Javier has often been utterly paralysed by his _____ fear of spiders.

15. In her newest film, the actor plays a heroine who is only pretending to be _____.

IX.3 For each of the following, select the one option from the choices on the right that is the correct synonym for the given word(s) in bold on the left.

1. **intercourse**   punctuation   altercation   interruption   conversation

2. **flighty**   sedate   unstable   airborne   unflappable

3. **pungent**   sweet-smelling   weak-smelling   strong-smelling   odourless

4. **morbid**   dreadful   obese   wholesome   malnourished

5. **hansom**   a handcart   a horse-drawn carriage used as a taxi   a wheelbarrow   a horse-drawn carriage used as a tram

6. **farrago**   confection   confusion   confrontation   conflation

7. **constrained**   loose   released   haphazard   restricted

8. **incipient rigour**   stiff neck   pins and needles   cold feet   goose pimples

9. **impediment**   improvement   obstacle   incentive   catalyst

10. **posture**   state   hypothesis   postilion   subterfuge

11. **capital**   centremost   rearmost   utmost   innermost

12. **whetted**   discharged   blunted   dulled   triggered

13. **constitution**   physical strength   mental strength   moral strength   character strength

14. **idiosyncratic**   generic   peculiar   intelligent   foolish

15. **appended**   ripped   layered   detached   added

Unit IX: Dr Lanyon's Narrative

accoutrement: outfit

misbegotten: contemptible

disparity: difference

sombre: desperate

pang: sensation

civilly: politely

convulsive: violent

minims: drops

effervesce: fizz

ebullition: bubbling

metamorphoses: transformations

parley: discussion

prodigy: wonder

transcendental: preternatural

turpitude: depravity

WHERE TO FIND THEM

The above words appear in the following section of 'Dr Lanyon's Narrative':

From the START of the paragraph that begins with

This person (who had thus, from the first moment of his entrance, struck in me what I can only describe as a disgustful curiosity)...

to the MIDDLE of the paragraph that begins with

What he told me in the next hour, I cannot bring my mind to set on paper. I saw what I saw, I heard what I heard...

BEFORE YOU START

Once you've reviewed the target words above, use this space to make a note of (i) all the words that you didn't know (before reading the meanings) and/or (ii) all the words you're uncertain about.

The words that you make a note of here are the words that you want to make sure that you've mastered by the time you get to the end of this part of the unit.

1. The word **parley** means **discussion**. _____

2. The word **prodigy** means **wonder**. _____

3. The word **turpitude** means **depravity**. _____

4. The word **disparity** means **outfit**. _____

5. The word **convulsive** means **politely**. _____

6. The word **misbegotten** means **violent**. _____

7. The word **minims** means **drops**. _____

8. The word **sombre** means **sensation**. _____

9. The word **accoutrement** means **desperate**. _____

10. The word **pang** means **difference**. _____

11. The word **effervesce** means **fizz**. _____

12. The word **transcendental** means **preternatural**. _____

13. The word **ebullition** means **bubbling**. _____

14. The word **civilly** means **contemptible**. _____

15. The word **metamorphoses** means **transformations**. _____

IX.5 For this exercise, you'll need to refer to your copy of *Dr Jekyll & Mr Hyde*. First, turn to 'Dr Lanyon's Narrative' and **find the paragraph that begins: 'I put him back, conscious at his touch of a certain icy pang…'**.

Once you've found the paragraph, start reading until you encounter each of the words in bold below. When you locate a word: **(a)** Write out the phrase, clause, or sentence in which it appears; and then **(b)** Rewrite the phrase, clause, or sentence and replace Stevenson's word with the meaning you've learnt. You may consult the text as often as you need to.

SAMPLE ANSWER:
1. ***feat***
*a. the **feat** was easy to Mr Utterson*
*b. the **endeavour** was easy to Mr Utterson*

1. **pang**

a. _____

b. _____

2. **civilly**

a. _____

b. _____

3. **convulsive**

a. _____

b. _____

4. **minims**

a. _____

b. _____

5. **effervesce**

a. _____

b. _____

IX.6 For the following, choose the one option from those listed that reflects the most correct meaning of the underlined word(s) as used by Stevenson in each of the given extracts below.

1. *the moral <u>turpitude</u> that man unveiled to me*
   a. wonder   b. transformation   c. depravity   d. politeness

2. *your sight shall be blasted by a <u>prodigy</u> to stagger the unbelief of Satan*
   a. contempt   b. violence   c. discussion   d. wonder

3. *will you suffer me [...] to go forth from your house without further <u>parley</u>?*
   a. violence   b. desperation   c. discussion   d. depravity

4. *My visitor was, indeed, on fire with <u>sombre</u> excitement*
   a. contemptible   b. polite   c. wonderful   d. desperate

5. *you who have denied the virtue of <u>transcendental</u> medicine*
   a. depraved   b. preternatural   c. contemptible   d. pious

6. *this fresh <u>disparity</u> seemed but to fit in with and to reinforce it*
   a. difference   b. politeness   c. violence   d. discussion

7. *there was something abnormal and <u>misbegotten</u> in the very essence of the creature*
   a. contemptible   b. unfamiliar   c. wonderful   d. heretical

8. *He thanked me with a smiling nod, measured out a few <u>minims</u>*
   a. bubbles   b. drops   c. slivers   d. shards

9. *the <u>ebullition</u> ceased and the compound changed to a dark purple*
   a. evaporation   b. distillation   c. filtering   d. bubbling

10. *"I beg your pardon, Dr Lanyon," he replied <u>civilly</u> enough*
    a. desperately   b. violently   c. politely   d. impolitely

11. *this ludicrous <u>accoutrement</u> was far from moving me to laughter*
    a. wonder   b. outfit   c. transformation   d. discussion

12. *I could hear his teeth grate with the <u>convulsive</u> action of his jaws*
    a. violent   b. abnormal   c. depraved   d. wonderful

13. *My visitor, who had watched these <u>metamorphoses</u> with a keen eye*
    a. wonders   b. discussions   c. outfits   d. transformations

Unit X: Dr Jekyll's Full Statement Of The Case

WORDS & MEANINGS ~ GROUP A

endowed: blessed

excellent parts: outstanding qualities

gaiety: liveliness

duplicity: deceitfulness

blazoned: boasted

exacting: demanding

aspirations: hopes

degradation: shame

trench: division

inverately: habitually

polity: group

denizens: people

infallibly: inevitably

radically: fundamentally

extraneous: separate

faggots: components

attired: clothed

agents: substances

aura: distinctive quality

effulgence: brilliance

WHERE TO FIND THEM

The above words appear in the following section of 'Dr Jekyll's Full Statement Of The Case':

From the START of the paragraph that begins with

I was born in the year 18— to a large fortune, endowed besides with excellent parts, inclined by nature to industry...

to the END of the paragraph that begins with

I was so far in my reflections when, as I have said, a side light began to shine upon the subject from the laboratory table...

BEFORE YOU START

Once you've reviewed the target words above, use this space to make a note of (i) all the words that you didn't know (before reading the meanings) and/or (ii) all the words you're uncertain about.

The words that you make a note of here are the words that you want to make sure that you've mastered by the time you get to the end of this part of the unit.

X.I Match the given words on the left to their correct meanings on the right. Then, use the letter to complete the definition statements below.

SAMPLE ANSWER: _Z is the meaning of **happy**_

Words	Meanings
endowed	A. shame
excellent parts	B. hopes
gaiety	C. components
duplicity	D. habitually
blazoned	E. substances
exacting	F. people
aspirations	G. blessed
degradation	H. separate
trench	I. brilliance
inverately	J. demanding
polity	K. clothed
denizens	L. outstanding qualities
infallibly	M. deceitfulness
radically	N. inevitably
extraneous	O. boasted
faggots	P. fundamentally
attired	Q. distinctive quality
agents	R. group
aura	S. division
effulgence	T. liveliness

1. ___ is the meaning of **endowed**.

2. ___ is the meaning of **excellent parts**.

3. ___ is the meaning of **gaiety**.

4. ___ is the meaning of **duplicity**.

5. ___ is the meaning of **blazoned**.

6. ___ is the meaning of **exacting**.

7. ___ is the meaning of **aspirations**.

8. ___ is the meaning of **degradation**.

9. ___ is the meaning of **trench**.

10. ___ is the meaning of **inverately**.

11. ___ is the meaning of **polity**.

12. ___ is the meaning of **denizens**.

13. ___ is the meaning of **infallibly**.

14. ___ is the meaning of **radically**.

15. ___ is the meaning of **extraneous**.

16. ___ is the meaning of **faggots**.

17. ___ is the meaning of **attired**.

18. ___ is the meaning of **agents**.

19. ___ is the meaning of **aura**.

20. ___ is the meaning of **effulgence**.

1. As a reward, the gods (blazoned / endowed / attired) the gift of invincibility upon the hero.

2. In fables, children who lie (exactingly / inverately / extraneously) tend to come to bad ends.

3. Over the last ten years, our city has (radically / duplicitously / degradingly) improved.

4. The memorial statue was notable for its (aura / gaiety / trench) of quiet dignity.

5. We must help the next generation fulfil their (aspirations / trenches / degradations).

6. Jon's (polity / excellent parts / duplicity) was finally exposed when Gina and I compared emails.

7. The terrified (agents / auras / denizens) of the city begged the dragon-slayer to help them.

8. Will we incur any (attired / endowed / extraneous) costs if we take out this loan?

9. The blacksmith bound the steel (faggots / denizens / aspirations) tightly in a bundle.

10. That was the most (extraneous / exacting / blazoned) course I've ever taken.

11. Recent political events have caused a (effulgence / aura / trench) to open up within my family.

12. We politely ask that you are suitably (exacting / attired / blazoned) for the event.

13. As more guests arrived, the (gaiety / agents / polity) in the ballroom began to rise.

14. Zara is trying to organize a (effulgence / aura / polity) of her fellow history students.

15. Two highly unstable chemical (aspirations / agents / denizens) are acrylic acid and vinyl acetate.

16. All the newspaper headlines (blazoned / attired / endowed) a single word: "VICTORY!"

17. The (denizens / effulgence / degradation) of the harvest moon left us all speechless.

18. Liam (extraneously / radically / infallibly) appears when there is free food on offer.

19. The (agents / effulgence / degradation) that followed his son's crime broke the merchant's heart.

20. "Mr Collins is a man of (duplicity / degradation / excellent parts)!" complimented Mrs Bennet.

1.	**gaiety**	uneasiness slipperiness weariness liveliness
2.	**denizens**	people dozens tourists demons
3.	**excellent parts**	remarkable roles superb chapters outstanding qualities fine sections
4.	**blazoned**	inflamed secreted boasted implicated
5.	**polity**	group courtesy politics chivalry
6.	**extraneous**	essential separate basic attached
7.	**aspirations**	enterprises methods doubts hopes
8.	**exacting**	calculating easy-going demanding bewildering
9.	**faggots**	compasses components composts companions
10.	**agents**	gentlemen substances agendum torments
11.	**inverately**	habitually occasionally chaotically unnervingly
12.	**attired**	exhausted clothed finalised stripped
13.	**trench**	unity division spanner fraction
14.	**endowed**	blessed dispossessed exhausted finalised
15.	**radically**	fundamentally partially superficially politically
16.	**effulgence**	opacity transparency stupidity brilliance
17.	**infallibly**	imprecisely immovably inevitably inaccurately
18.	**aura**	humorous quality annoying quality sinful quality distinctive quality
19.	**duplicity**	replication subservience deceitfulness criticism
20.	**degradation**	rage humility admiration shame

Unit X: Dr Jekyll's Full Statement Of The Case

Words & Meanings ~ Group B

scruple: small amount
immaterial tabernacle: soul
racking: agonising
recklessness: rashness
millrace: torrent
exulting: glorying
constellations: stars
vigilance: watchfulness
efficacy: power
repugnance: disgust

dissolution: change
diabolical: satanic
aversions: distaste
incoherency: inconsistency
unscrupulous: unprincipled
parry: fend off
pecuniary: financial
bravos: thugs
vicarious: second-hand
depravity: wickedness

Where To Find Them

The above words appear in the following section of 'Dr Jekyll's Full Statement Of The Case':

From the START of the paragraph that begins with

I hesitated long before I put this theory to the test of practice. I knew well that I risked death...

to the MIDDLE of the paragraph that begins with

The pleasures which I made haste to seek in my disguise were, as I have said, undignified; I would scarce use a harder term...

Before You Start

Once you've reviewed the target words above, use this space to make a note of (i) all the words that you didn't know (before reading the meanings) and/or (ii) all the words you're uncertain about.

The words that you make a note of here are the words that you want to make sure that you've mastered by the time you get to the end of this part of the unit.

1. The words **immaterial tabernacle** mean **soul**. _____

2. The word **dissolution** means **unprincipled**. _____

3. The word **efficacy** means **thugs**. _____

4. The word **vicarious** means **satanic**. _____

5. The word **repugnance** means **wickedness**. _____

6. The word **vigilance** means **watchfulness**. _____

7. The word **bravos** means **change**. _____

8. The word **diabolical** means **financial**. _____

9. The word **millrace** means **torrent**. _____

10. The word **exulting** means **glorying**. _____

11. The word **depravity** means **distaste**. _____

12. The word **incoherency** means **second-hand**. _____

13. The word **scruple** means **small amount**. _____

14. The word **recklessness** means **rashness**. _____

15. The word **parry** means **power**. _____

16. The word **unscrupulous** means **disgust**. _____

17. The word **pecuniary** means **inconsistency**. _____

18. The word **constellations** means **stars**. _____

19. The word **aversions** means **fend off**. _____

20. The word **racking** means **agonising**. _____

X.5 For this exercise, you'll need to refer to your copy of *Dr Jekyll & Mr Hyde.* First, turn to 'Dr Jekyll's Full Statement Of The Case' and **find the paragraph that begins: 'There was no mirror, at that date...'.**

Once you've found the paragraph, start reading until you encounter each of the words in bold below. When you locate a word: **(a)** Write out the phrase, clause, or sentence in which it appears; and then **(b)** Rewrite the phrase, clause, or sentence and replace Stevenson's word with the meaning you've learnt. You may consult the text as often as you need to.

SAMPLE ANSWER:
1. feat
a. the feat was easy to Mr Utterson
b. the endeavour was easy to Mr Utterson

1. **vigilance**

a. _____

b. _____

2. **efficacy**

a. _____

b. _____

3. **repugnance**

a. _____

b. _____

4. **dissolution**

a. _____

b. _____

5. **diabolical**

a. _____

b. _____

1. *this <u>incoherency</u> of my life was daily growing more unwelcome*
   a. watchfulness   b. wickedness   c. second-handedness   d. inconsistency

2. *a creature whom I knew well to be silent and <u>unscrupulous</u>*
   a. unprincipled   b. watchful   c. inconsistent   d. powerful

3. *that <u>immaterial tabernacle</u> which I looked to it to change*
   a. principle   b. body   c. law   d. soul

4. *their unsleeping <u>vigilance</u>*
   a. power   b. watchfulness   c. torrents   d. principles

5. *a current of disordered sensual images running like a <u>millrace</u> in my fancy*
   a. dream   b. torrent   c. power   d. nightmare

6. *and to <u>parry</u> mishaps, I even called and made myself a familiar object*
   a. fend off   b. ensure   c. watch   d. measure

7. *Men have before hired <u>bravos</u> to transact their crimes*
   a. friends   b. bankers   c. thugs   d. accountants

8. *the least <u>scruple</u> of an overdose*
   a. moral   b. power   c. small amount   d. doubt

9. *I was often plunged into a kind of wonder at my <u>vicarious</u> depravity*
   a. agonising   b. torrential   c. second-hand   d. financial

10. *The most <u>racking</u> pangs succeeded*
    a. inconsistent   b. agonising   c. wicked   d. torrential

11. *I was often plunged into a kind of wonder at my vicarious <u>depravity</u>*
    a. power   b. wickedness   c. agony   d. principles

12. *I could enter on that of Edward Hyde without <u>pecuniary</u> loss*
    a. financial   b. second-hand   c. agonising   d. inconsistent

13. *The evil side of my nature, to which I had now transferred the stamping <u>efficacy</u>*
    a. wickedness   b. inconsistency   c. power   d. duality

WORDS & MEANINGS ~ GROUP C

familiar: demon

inherently: intrinsically

malign: evil

insidiously: craftily

connived: colluded

chastisement: punishment

comely: pleasing

swart: swarthy

anatomical theatre: dissecting room

projecting: putting forth

gusto: relish

faculties: mental powers

suffer: agonize

inducements: temptations

obliterate: destroy

throes: violent spasms

unbridled: uncontrolled

propensity: tendency

provocation: cause for anger

mauled: savaged

WHERE TO FIND THEM

The above words appear in the following section of 'Dr Jekyll's Full Statement Of The Case':

From the MIDDLE of the paragraph that begins with

The pleasures which I made haste to seek in my disguise were, as I have said, undignified; I would scarce use a harder term...

to the START of the paragraph that begins with

Instantly the spirit of hell awoke in me and raged. With a transport of glee, I mauled the unresisting body, tasting delight from every blow...

BEFORE YOU START

Once you've reviewed the target words above, use this space to make a note of (i) all the words that you didn't know (before reading the meanings) and/or (ii) all the words you're uncertain about.

The words that you make a note of here are the words that you want to make sure that you've mastered by the time you get to the end of this part of the unit.

familiar	1. relish	_____
Inherently	2. putting forth	_____
malign	3. uncontrolled	_____
insidiously	4. intrinsically	_____
connived	5. violent spasms	_____
chastisement	6. colluded	_____
comely	7. evil	_____
swart	8. tendency	_____
anatomical theatre	9. demon	_____
projecting	10. swarthy	_____
gusto	11. savaged	_____
faculties	12. dissecting room	_____
suffer	13. pleasing	_____
inducements	14. mental powers	_____
obliterate	15. punishment	_____
throes	16. craftily	_____
unbridled	17. cause for anger	_____
propensity	18. agonize	_____
provocation	19. destroy	_____
mauled	20. temptations	_____

1. Ivy's (chastisement / throes / inducements) for breaking that vase was disproportionate.

2. A group of northern noblemen (connived / mauled / unbridled) to discredit the queen.

3. Her analytical (throes / faculties / chastisements) have become quite formidable.

4. The verb 'to (suffer / malign / obliterate)' can mean 'to undergo' or 'to allow'.

5. "I believe Tina is an (insidiously / comely / inherently) good person," Betty said stoutly.

6. "What (provocations / inducements / faculties) can I offer you to stay?" the banker asked the client.

7. The prophecy warned of the arrival of a (connived / malign / projecting) stranger.

8. As the poison spread, the prince collapsed in (inducements / throes / provocations) of agony.

9. Be careful: the slightest (projecting / propensity / provocation) sets Xavier off.

10. Priscilla was a (mauled / connived / comely) young woman, graced with a cheery disposition.

11. The twins were brimming with (malign / mauled / unbridled) pride at winning the competition.

12. "The widespread (chastisement / faculties / projecting) of this lie is unacceptable," fumed Ivor.

13. When he was a young man, my uncle was badly (maligned / mauled / unbridled) by a bear.

14. "I will send you a (malign / familiar / swart) to do your bidding," the wizard promised the witch.

15. Theo has a (propensity / provocation / projecting) to believe outlandish conspiracy theories.

16. Mr Bumble smacked his lips with (gusto / chastisement / provocation) when he saw the meal.

17. The (anatomical theatre / projecting / faculties) was a feature of early modern European universities.

18. The tyrant threatened to (unbridle / suffer / obliterate) the city if it did not yield to his demands.

19. A common stereotype in romantic fiction is the (gusto / mauled / swart), mysterious hero.

20. (Inherently / Comely / Insidiously), the spy worked his way into the highest circles of the government.

For each of the following, select the one option from the choices on the right that is the correct synonym for the given word(s) in bold on the left.

1. **suffer** | disallow   agonize   restore   intimidate

2. **propensity** | dislike   apathy   tendency   devotion

3. **mauled** | petted   wailed   savaged   tamed

4. **faculties** | political powers   mental powers   social powers   legal powers

5. **familiar** | newcomer   demon   stranger   witch

6. **provocation** | cause for anger   cause for hunger   cause for laziness   cause for laughter

7. **insidiously** | blamelessly   inwardly   necessarily   craftily

8. **inherently** | unnaturally   intrinsically   artificially   explicitly

9. **swart** | worthy   swampy   warty   swarthy

10. **inducements** | temptations   reductions   trials   emotions

11. **comely** | plain-looking   welcoming   unsatisfying   pleasing

12. **malign** | genial   magnanimous   evil   saintly

13. **connived** | condemned   raged   deviated   colluded

14. **anatomical theatre** | drawing room   darkroom   card room   dissecting room

15. **obliterate** | devour   renovate   misread   destroy

16. **unbridled** | uncontrolled   temperate   riderless   single

17. **throes** | vacant looks   valid moves   violent spasms   valiant attempts

18. **projecting** | recalling hence   withdrawing forthwith   pulling toward   putting forth

19. **chastisement** | forgiveness   punishment   chastity   abridgement

20. **gusto** | relish   apathy   distaste   friction

WORDS & MEANINGS ~ GROUP D

delirium: derangement

self-indulgence: unrestrained self-gratification

rent: ripped

renunciation: forsaking

condescension: scorn

vainglorious: overly proud

quarry: prey

succumbed: surrendered

consign: send

rifle: ransack

obsequiously: slavishly

abhorrence: loathing

the gallows: execution by hanging

prostration: exhaustion

premonitory: warning

languidly: sickly

poignant: wretched

amorphous: unshaped

usurp: supplant

scaffold: platform for execution

WHERE TO FIND THEM

The above words appear in the following section of 'Dr Jekyll's Full Statement Of The Case':

From the START of the paragraph that begins with

Instantly the spirit of hell awoke in me and raged. With a transport of glee, I mauled the unresisting body, tasting delight from every blow...

to the END of the paragraph that begins with

About a week has passed, and I am now finishing this statement under the influence of the last of the old powders...

BEFORE YOU START

Once you've reviewed the target words above, use this space to make a note of (i) all the words that you didn't know (before reading the meanings) and/or (ii) all the words you're uncertain about.

The words that you make a note of here are the words that you want to make sure that you've mastered by the time you get to the end of this part of the unit.

1. The word **usurp** means **supplant**. _____

2. The word **vainglorious** means **scorn**. _____

3. The word **abhorrence** means **ransack**. _____

4. The word **languidly** means **sickly**. _____

5. The word **condescension** means **derangement**. _____

6. The word **delirium** means **prey**. _____

7. The word **premonitory** means **warning**. _____

8. The word **self-indulgence** means **loathing**. _____

9. The word **consign** means **surrendered**. _____

10. The word **succumbed** means **unrestrained self-gratification**. _____

11. The word **poignant** means **wretched**. _____

12. The word **obsequiously** means **forsaking**. _____

13. The word **prostration** means **exhaustion**. _____

14. The word **renunciation** means **ripped**. _____

15. The word **quarry** means **send**. _____

16. The word **scaffold** means **platform for execution**. _____

17. The word **rent** means **overly proud**. _____

18. The word **rifle** means **slavishly**. _____

19. The words **the gallows** mean **execution by hanging**. _____

20. The word **amorphous** means **unshaped**. _____

A. respect — esteem — admiration — approbation

The word _____ is an antonym of all the above words.

B. lucidity — reason — balance — rationality

The word _____ is an antonym of all the above words.

C. relinquish — surrender — abdicate — cede

The word _____ is an antonym of all the above words.

D. indulgence — participation — licensing — humouring

The word _____ is an antonym of all the above words.

E. abstinence — moderation — frugality — temperance

The word _____ is an antonym of all the above words.

F. appetite — fondness — preference — relish

The word _____ is an antonym of all the above words.

G. resisted — conquered — withstood — combated

The word _____ is an antonym of all the above words.

H. humble — modest — unpretentious — unassuming

The word _____ is an antonym of all the above words.

I. formed — moulded — structured — shaped

The word _____ is an antonym of all the above words.

J. vigorously — healthily — sturdily — robustly

The word _____ is an antonym of all the above words.

1. *where Jekyll perhaps might have <u>succumbed</u>, Hyde rose*
   a. scorned   b. supplanted   c. surrendered   d. warned

2. *with what sincere <u>renunciation</u> I locked the door*
   a. warning   b. forsaking   c. derangement   d. scorn

3. *This was the shocking thing [...] that the <u>amorphous</u> dust gesticulated and sinned*
   a. unshaped   b. scornful   c. sickly   d. wretched

4. *emptied by fever, <u>languidly</u> weak both in body and mind*
   a. sleeplessly   b. wretchedly   c. worryingly   d. sickly

5. *At all hours of the day and night, I would be taken with the <u>premonitory</u> shudder*
   a. chilling   b. annoying   c. shaking   d. warning

6. *I slept after the <u>prostration</u> of the day*
   a. derangement   b. wretchedness   c. exhaustion   d. surrender

7. *not a look did they exchange in my presence; but <u>obsequiously</u> took my orders*
   a. wretchedly   b. slavishly   c. proudly   d. scornfully

8. *the most <u>poignant</u> part of his distress*
   a. impolite   b. deranged   c. wretched   d. forsaken

9. *at the very moment of that <u>vainglorious</u> thought, a qualm came over me*
   a. overly proud   b. warning   c. deranged   d. sickly

10. *that what was dead, and had no shape, should <u>usurp</u> the offices of life*
    a. scorn   b. exhaust   c. warn   d. supplant

11. *this brief <u>condescension</u> to my evil finally destroyed the balance of my soul*
    a. surrender   b. scorn   c. warning   d. exhilaration

12. *my own servants would <u>consign</u> me to the gallows*
    a. beg   b. send   c. encourage   d. ask

13. *I was suddenly, in the top fit of my <u>delirium</u>, struck through the heart by a cold thrill*
    a. scorn   b. pride   c. exhaustion   d. derangement

SCAVENGER HUNT #1: STORY OF THE DOOR

Turn to your copy of *Jekyll and Hyde* and find the extract that starts with **'"Well, it was this way," returned Mr. Enfield...'** and ends with **'...The cheque was genuine.'**

Read the extract carefully, then, come back to this page to see what you need to search for. Log your findings in the correct boxes below. **NB**: <u>the clues are listed sequentially</u> (i.e. they follow the order of the solutions as they appear in the text). You may consult the text as often as you need to.

A. A single word meaning **walking noisily and stiffly**

B. 3 consecutive words meaning **an intersecting or connecting street**

C. A single word used to indicate **an exclamation**

D. A simile used to describe **an undemonstrative disposition**

E. 4 consecutive words meaning **to ruin a person's reputation**

F. A single word meaning **a person's reputation**

G. A simile that **draws on figures from Greek mythology**

H. 3 consecutive words meaning **to gain financially**

I. 4 consecutive words meaning **desired to resist**

J. 4 consecutive words meaning **a large, unspecified amount of money**

Scavenger Hunt #11: Search For Mr Hyde

Turn to your copy of *Jekyll and Hyde* and find the extract that starts with **'And at last his patience was rewarded...'** and ends with **'...that of your new friend.'"**

Read the extract carefully, then, come back to this page to see what you need to search for. Log your findings in the correct boxes below. **NB**: <u>the clues are listed sequentially</u> (i.e. they follow the order of the solutions as they appear in the text). You may consult the text as often as you need to.

A. A simile that **draws on dancing**

B. A metaphor that **compares London to an animal**

C. 3 consecutive words that combine **low and steady sounds with rattling sounds**

D. A single word meaning **became greater in intensity**

E. A metaphor that **draws on serpents**

F. 2 consecutive words meaning **quite determinedly**

G. 2 consecutive words meaning **appropriate speech**

H. 2 consecutive alliterative words meaning **a deadly combination**

I. 2 consecutive alliterative words meaning **barely mortal**

J. 2 consecutive sibilant words that **emphasise the presence of evil**

Turn to your copy of *Jekyll and Hyde* and find the extract that starts with **'A fortnight later...'** and ends with **'...we had agreed to drop.'"**

Read the extract carefully, then, come back to this page to see what you need to search for. Log your findings in the correct boxes below. **NB**: the clues are listed sequentially (i.e. they follow the order of the solutions as they appear in the text). You may consult the text as often as you need to.

A. A single word meaning **a large indefinite number**

B. A verb meaning **to hold a person back / to claim a person's attention**

C. 3 consecutive words meaning **becoming clear-headed**

D. A single word meaning **ability**

E. A single word meaning **harboured**

F. A single word that refers to **the second of two things mentioned**

G. 3 consecutive words meaning **an attentive onlooker**

H. 4 consecutive words meaning **dismissed (something) casually**

I. A single word that means **without compassion or pity**

J. 7 consecutive words indicating **a darkening facial expression**

Scavenger Hunt #IV: The Carew Murder Case

Turn to your copy of *Jekyll and Hyde* and find the extract that starts with **'Nearly a year later...'** and ends with **'...showed the broken stick.'**

Read the extract carefully, then, come back to this page to see what you need to search for. Log your findings in the correct boxes below. **NB**: the clues are listed sequentially (i.e. they follow the order of the solutions as they appear in the text). You may consult the text as often as you need to.

A. A single word meaning **thought / reflection**

B. 2 consecutive words meaning **approaching**

C. 4 consecutive words meaning **were close enough to talk**

D. A single word meaning **became pregnant OR formed**

E. 2 consecutive words meaning **behaving (informal)**

F. An **animal simile**

G. A 4-word metaphor comparing **physical assault to a severe weather event**

H. A single word referring to **the low area at the side of a street to carry off water**

I. A single old-fashioned word meaning **to where**

J. A sentence meaning **something will be much talked about**

Turn to your copy of *Jekyll and Hyde* and find the extract that starts with **'Presently after, he sat...'** and ends with **'...shape his future course.'**

Read the extract carefully, then, come back to this page to see what you need to search for. Log your findings in the correct boxes below. **NB**: <u>the clues are listed sequentially</u> (i.e. they follow the order of the solutions as they appear in the text). You may consult the text as often as you need to.

A. A single word meaning **precisely**

B. A single word meaning **kept in the dark**

C. A metaphor that **draws on the idea of a resting bird**

D. 4 consecutive words that **form a simile AND which are alliterative**

E. A single obsolete word meaning **dissolved**

F. A single word meaning **to thin out and make disappear**

G. A single word meaning **gradually**

H. A single word meaning **relaxed**

I. A single word meaning **helpful**

J. 4 consecutive words meaning **determine his subsequent actions**

Scavenger Hunt #VI: Incident Of Dr Lanyon

Turn to your copy of *Jekyll and Hyde* and find the extract that starts with **'As soon as he got home...'** and ends with **'...of his private safe.'**

Read the extract carefully, then, come back to this page to see what you need to search for. Log your findings in the correct boxes below. **NB**: <u>the clues are listed sequentially</u> (i.e. they follow the order of the solutions as they appear in the text). You may consult the text as often as you need to.

A. A single word meaning **barring**

B. A single word meaning **unable to be changed**

C. A single word meaning **from this point on**

D. An example of **parallelism**

E. A single word meaning **emasculating**

F. A verb meaning **to ease**

G. An example of **personification that draws on sadness**

H. A single word meaning **written on the cover / outside of something**

I. A single word meaning **joined**

J. A single word meaning **duties**

Scavenger Hunt #VII: Incident At The Window

Turn to your copy of *Jekyll and Hyde* and find the extract that starts with **"'It was impossible...'** and ends with **'...in their eyes.'**

Read the extract carefully, then, come back to this page to see what you need to search for. Log your findings in the correct boxes below. **NB**: the clues are listed sequentially (i.e. they follow the order of the solutions as they appear in the text). You may consult the text as often as you need to.

A. A single word meaning **a fool**

B. 3 consecutive words meaning **discovered**

C. A single word meaning **yard**

D. A verb meaning **hope**

E. An example of **repetition**

F. 4 consecutive words meaning **go for a brisk walk**

G. 4 consecutive words meaning **the rooms are a mess**

H. 4 consecutive words meaning **erased / removed**

I. A single word meaning **a momentary view**

J. A single word meaning **corresponding**

SCAVENGER HUNT #VIII: THE LAST NIGHT

Turn to your copy of *Jekyll and Hyde* and find the extract that starts with **'Poole swung the axe...'** and ends with **'...the body of your master.'"**

Read the extract carefully, then, come back to this page to see what you need to search for. Log your findings in the correct boxes below. **NB**: <u>the clues are listed sequentially</u> (i.e. they follow the order of the solutions as they appear in the text). You may consult the text as often as you need to.

A. A single word meaning **complete / utter**

B. A single word meaning **dismayed / shocked**

C. A single word meaning **loud noise**

D. A single word meaning **followed**

E. 3 examples of **personification in a single sentence**

F. A single word meaning **ordinary**

G. A single word meaning **severely**

H. A single word meaning **gazed upon**

I. A single word meaning **a suicide**

J. A single word meaning **final judgement**

SCAVENGER HUNT #IX: DR LANYON'S NARRATIVE

Turn to your copy of *Jekyll and Hyde* and find the extract that starts with **'"Sir," said I...'** and ends with **'...Hastie Lanyon.'**

Read the extract carefully, then, come back to this page to see what you need to search for. Log your findings in the correct boxes below. **NB**: <u>the clues are listed sequentially</u> (i.e. they follow the order of the solutions as they appear in the text). You may consult the text as often as you need to.

A. A single word meaning **feigning**

B. A single word meaning **calmness**

C. A single word meaning **incapable of being accounted for**

D. A single word meaning **promises**

E. A single word meaning **ridiculed / scorned**

F. An example of **a tricolon (i.e. rule of 3)**

G. A single word meaning **blood-shot**

H. A simile that **draws on resurrection**

I. A single word meaning **sceptical**

J. A single word meaning **sorrow for faults or sins**

Scavenger Hunt #X: Dr Jekyll's Full Statement Of The Case

Turn to your copy of *Jekyll and Hyde* and find the extract that starts with **'I was stepping leisurely across...'** and ends with **'...lent efficacy to the draught.'**

Read the extract carefully, then, come back to this page to see what you need to search for. Log your findings in the correct boxes below. **NB**: the clues are listed sequentially (i.e. they follow the order of the solutions as they appear in the text). You may consult the text as often as you need to.

A. A single word meaning **signalled the approach of**

B. A single word meaning **bring back to an original or former state**

C. 2 consecutive words meaning **imminent terrible fate**

D. A metaphor that **draws on heat and water**

E. A single word meaning **a joint inheritor**

F. A single word meaning **made motions while speaking**

G. A single word meaning **rebellious**

H. An **animal simile**

I. 2 consecutive words meaning **destroyed himself**

J. 3 consecutive words meaning **submission to hopelessness**

UNIT I: STORY OF THE DOOR

I.1 Definitions Completion
(1) T
(2) L
(3) H
(4) P
(5) M
(6) D
(7) R
(8) K
(9) C
(10) J
(11) S
(12) N
(13) I
(14) O
(15) G
(16) F
(17) B
(18) A
(19) Q
(20) E

I.2 Cloze Test
(1) thoroughfare
(2) countenance
(3) passage
(4) emulously
(5) chanced
(6) vintages
(7) mortify
(8) singularly
(9) in coquetry
(10) rugged
(11) kinsman
(12) beaconed
(13) eminently
(14) florid
(15) catholicity
(16) rambles
(17) heresy
(18) chambers
(19) dusty
(20) austere

I.3 Synonyms
(1) shone
(2) expensive wines
(3) happened
(4) customers
(5) office
(6) distinctly
(7) face
(8) uninteresting
(9) strict

(10) road
(11) extremely
(12) relative
(13) suppress
(14) broad-mindedness
(15) unconventional opinion
(16) attractively
(17) competitively
(18) stony
(19) walks
(20) flamboyant

I.4 Definitions Assessment
(1) True
(2) False
(3) True
(4) False
(5) False
(6) False
(7) True
(8) False
(9) False
(10) True
(11) False
(12) True
(13) True
(14) True
(15) False
(16) True
(17) True
(18) False
(19) False
(20) True

I.5 Word Webs
Answers will vary.

Possible Answers for "Juggernaut":
- *Event(s): Trampling of the Girl*
- *Character(s): Hyde; Enfield; Unnamed Girl*
- *Location(s): A London by-street*
- *Theme(s): physical violence*
- *Context(s): the Victorian poor; class conflict*
- *Quote(s): "wasn't like a man"*
- *Motif(s)/Symbol(s): (in)humanity*

Possible Answers for "Sawbones":
- *Event(s): Trampling of the Girl*
- *Character(s): Enfield; Hyde; Sawbones/Apothecary/Doctor*
- *Location(s): A London by-street*
- *Theme(s): social responsibility*
- *Context(s): science & medicine in the Victorian era*
- *Quote(s): "as emotional as a bagpipe"*
- *Motif(s)/Symbol(s): the scientist*

Possible Answers for "proprieties":
- *Event(s): Jekyll's signature on the cheque*
- *Character(s): Jekyll; Hyde; Utterson; Enfield*
- *Location(s): The cellar door*
- *Theme(s): appearance vs reality; duality; duplicity*
- *Context(s): social respectability; the Victorian gentleman*
- *Quote(s): "the very pink of proprieties"*
- *Motif(s)/Symbol(s): the door*

I.6 Cloze Test
(1) gable
(2) harpies
(3) pedantically
(4) vein
(5) sawbones
(6) cane
(7) ravages
(8) apothecary
(9) partakes too much of
(10) delicacy
(11) mouldings
(12) Queer Street
(13) capers
(14) passenger
(15) distained
(16) proprieties
(17) apocryphal
(18) collared
(19) Juggernaut
(20) screwed

UNIT II: SEARCH FOR MR HYDE

II.1 Matching Words to Meanings
(1) religious writer = divinity
(2) was based = reposed
(3) fortress = citadel
(4) lively = boisterous
(5) burden = burthen
(6) devil = fiend
(7) qualities = attributes
(8) offensive = obnoxious
(9) handwritten = holograph
(10) death = decease
(11) perturbed = baffled
(12) marked = endorsed
(13) determined = decided
(14) friendliness = geniality
(15) well-dressed = dapper
(16) appearance = presentment
(17) previously = hitherto
(18) dull = dry
(19) financial supporter =

benefactor
(20) irritant = eyesore

II.2 Synonyms
(1) perturbed
(2) well-dressed
(3) determined
(4) qualities
(5) appearance
(6) financial supporter
(7) religious writer
(8) handwritten
(9) previously
(10) offensive
(11) lively
(12) burden
(13) irritant
(14) was based
(15) death
(16) dull
(17) fortress
(18) friendliness
(19) marked
(20) devil

II.3 Cloze Test
(1) baffled
(2) decease
(3) decided
(4) holograph
(5) dry
(6) attributes
(7) divinity
(8) reposed
(9) fiend
(10) endorsed
(11) eyesore
(12) boisterous
(13) Citadel
(14) hitherto
(15) geniality
(16) dapper
(17) presentment
(18) obnoxious
(19) burthen
(20) benefactor

II.4 Definitions Completion
(1) B
(2) D
(3) T
(4) I
(5) E
(6) N
(7) F
(8) J
(9) R
(10) A
(11) L

(12) H
(13) M
(14) P
(15) Q
(16) C
(17) K
(18) G
(19) S
(20) O

II.5 Find & Rephrase
Answers may vary. Suggested answers:

(1) composure
• a. gave his friend a few seconds to recover his <u>composure</u>
• b. gave his friend a few seconds to recover his <u>calmness</u>
(2) protégé
• a. Did you ever come across a <u>protégé</u> of his—one Hyde?
• b. Did you ever come across a <u>student</u> of his—one Hyde?
(3) besieged
• a. <u>besieged</u> by questions
• b. <u>overwhelmed</u> by questions
(4) dwelling
• a. near to Mr. Utterson's <u>dwelling</u>
• b. near to Mr. Utterson's <u>house</u>
(5) gross
• a. tossed in the <u>gross</u> darkness of the night
• b. tossed in the <u>total</u> darkness of the night

II.6 Cloze Test
(1) protégé
(2) footfalls
(3) composure
(4) besieged
(5) prevision
(6) bowels of mercy
(7) quaint
(8) conveyancing
(9) estranged
(10) fanciful
(11) bondage
(12) apropos
(13) bidding
(14) concourse
(15) Damon and Pythias
(16) inordinate
(17) balderdash
(18) gross
(19) dwelling
(20) arrested

II.7 Definitions Assessment
(1) True
(2) False
(3) True
(4) True
(5) False
(6) False
(7) False
(8) False
(9) True
(10) False
(11) True
(12) True
(13) True
(14) False
(15) False
(16) True
(17) False
(18) False
(19) True
(20) True

II.8 Antonyms
A. troglodytic
B. brooded
C. condoned
D. iniquity
E. timidity
F. apprehension
G. malformation
H. perplexity

II.9 Cloze Test
(1) dissecting room
(2) flags
(3) wont
(4) disquietude
(5) conceived
(6) timidity
(7) clay continent
(8) apprehension
(9) perplexity
(10) statute of limitations
(11) condoned
(12) fanlight
(13) transfigures
(14) cabinets
(15) brooded
(16) *pede claudo*
(17) iniquity
(18) troglodytic
(19) transpires
(20) malformation

Unit III: Dr Jekyll Was Quite At Ease

III.1 Matching Meanings to Words
(1) a. a trifle
(2) c. threshold
(3) d. make a clean breast of
(4) b. loose-tongued
(5) b. unobtrusive
(6) a. hide-bound
(7) c. cronies
(8) d. abominable
(9) b. blatant
(10) a. contrived
(11) a. pedant
(12) d. downright
(13) b. incoherency of manner
(14) c. irrepressible

III.2 Find & Rephrase
Answers may vary. Suggested answers:

(1) abominable
- a. "What I heard was <u>abominable</u>," said Utterson.
- b. "What I heard was <u>loathsome</u>," said Utterson.

(2) incoherency of manner
- a. with a certain <u>incoherency of manner</u>
- b. with a certain <u>hysteria</u>

(3) make a clean breast of
- a. <u>Make a clean breast of</u> this in confidence
- b. <u>Confess</u> this in confidence

(4) downright
- a. this is <u>downright</u> good of you
- b. this is <u>absolutely</u> good of you

(5) irrepressible
- a. Utterson heaved an <u>irrepressible</u> sigh
- b. Utterson heaved an <u>uncontrollable</u> sigh

III.3 Words & Meanings in Context
(1) b. purist
(2) a. unashamed
(3) d. confess
(4) c. arranged
(5) b. doorstep
(6) a. friends
(7) c. hysteria
(8) d. talkative
(9) b. loathsome
(10) a. conservative

(11) a. a little
(12) b. restrained
(13) c. uncontrollable

Unit IV: The Carew Murder Case

IV.1 Definitions Completion
(1) G
(2) O
(3) I
(4) F
(5) A
(6) H
(7) E
(8) M
(9) N
(10) J
(11) D
(12) L
(13) C
(14) B
(15) K

IV.2 Synonyms
(1) fire
(2) playing
(3) waving
(4) blowing away
(5) senseless
(6) intense
(7) dark cloud
(8) exceptional
(9) colours
(10) made
(11) height
(12) injured
(13) where
(14) recoiled
(15) approached

IV.3 Words & Meanings in Context
(1) b. approached
(2) b. blowing away
(3) b. exceptional
(4) a. recoiled
(5) d. intense
(6) c. made
(7) c. dark cloud
(8) b. injured
(9) d. senseless
(10) a. playing
(11) a. waving
(12) d. height
(13) d. fire

IV.4 Matching Words to Meanings
(1) unearthed = disinterred
(2) searched = ransacked
(3) expert judge = connoisseur
(4) pub = gin palace
(5) unpleasant = odious
(6) insincerity = hypocrisy
(7) lit = kindled
(8) runaway = fugitive
(9) friends = familiars
(10) fireplace = hearth
(11) attack = assail
(12) household linen = napery
(13) scruffy = slatternly
(14) disreputable = blackguardly
(15) dark (brown) pigment = umber

IV.5 Word Webs
Answers will vary.

Possible Answers for "assail":
- *Event(s): Sir Danvers Carew's murder*
- *Character(s): Hyde; Sir Danvers Carew; The Maid*
- *Location(s): Soho*
- *Theme(s): murder; violence (verbal & physical); order vs chaos*
- *Context(s): Charles Darwin & The Origin of the Species*
- *Quote(s): "ape-like fury"*
- *Motif(s)/Symbol(s): cane*

Possible Answers for "hypocrisy":
- *Event(s): Utterson & Inspector Newcomen's inspection of Hyde's rooms*
- *Character(s): Hyde's housekeeper; Utterson; Inspector Newcomen*
- *Location(s): Mr Hyde's house*
- *Theme(s): duality; deception; (dis)loyalty*
- *Context(s): Victorian societal norms; Victorian social hierarchy (masters/mistresses & servants)*
- *Quote(s): "A flash of odious joy"*
- *Motif(s)/Symbol(s): rooms & interiors*

Possible Answers for "familiars":
- *Event(s): Discovery of Hyde's isolation*
- *Character(s): Hyde*
- *Location(s): Soho*
- *Theme(s): male friendship; solitude vs companionship*

- *Context(s): Victorian bachelorhood/gentleman*
- *Quote(s): "haunting sense of unexpressed deformity"*
- *Motif(s)/Symbol(s): money*

IV.6 Words & Meanings in Context
(1) d. unpleasant
(2) d. fireplace
(3) b. runaway
(4) d. friends
(5) c. expert judge
(6) c. lit
(7) b. attack
(8) a. searched
(9) c. unearthed
(10) a. dark (brown) pigment
(11) b. disreputable
(12) c. scruffy
(13) b. household linen

Unit V: Incident Of The Letter

V.1 Definitions Assessment
(1) False
(2) True
(3) True
(4) False
(5) True
(6) False
(7) True
(8) False
(9) False
(10) True
(11) False
(12) False
(13) False
(14) False
(15) False
(16) True
(17) True
(18) False
(19) False
(20) True

V.2 Synonyms
(1) fit
(2) accommodation
(3) generated
(4) red gems
(5) speech
(6) small private room
(7) woollen cloth
(8) thought
(9) the law
(10) upright tilting mirror

(11) cupboards
(12) meticulously
(13) reddish-purple
(14) relating to the body
(15) stated
(16) difficult
(17) advertisements
(18) domed skylight
(19) whirlpool
(20) empty

V.3 Cloze Test
(1) carbuncles
(2) ruminated
(3) elicited
(4) cabinet
(5) cupola
(6) signified
(7) circulars
(8) quarters
(9) cheval glass
(10) presses
(11) Counsel
(12) oration
(13) gaunt
(14) imperial
(15) baize
(16) qualm
(17) anatomical
(18) eddy
(19) ticklish
(20) sedulously

Unit VI: Incident Of Dr Lanyon

VI.1 Matching Words to Meanings
(1) direction = tenor
(2) strict = stringent
(3) damned = accursed
(4) erased = blotted out
(5) knowledge = ken
(6) regarded negatively = resented
(7) cold-hearted = callous
(8) uneasy = disquieted
(9) enigmatic = inscrutable
(10) allow = suffer
(11) imprisonment = bondage
(12) hermit = recluse
(13) isolation = seclusion
(14) decreased = fell off
(15) meaning = drift
(16) friendships = amities
(17) uncovered = unearthed
(18) death sentence = death warrant
(19) scandalous = disreputable

(20) executor = trustee

VI.2 Cloze Test
(1) inscrutable
(2) disquieted
(3) bondage
(4) drift
(5) recluse
(6) blotted out
(7) seclusion
(8) unearthed
(9) suffer
(10) stringent
(11) resented
(12) tenor
(13) trustee
(14) accursed
(15) amities
(16) callous
(17) fell off
(18) disreputable
(19) ken
(20) death warrant

VI.3 Antonyms
A. disquieted
B. stringent
C. accursed
D. suffer
E. resented
F. inscrutable
G. disreputable
H. callous

Unit VII: Incident At The Window

VII.1 Matching Meanings to Words
(1) c. stirrings
(2) b. circulation
(3) c. presence
(4) b. mien
(5) a. repulsion
(6) a. whipping up
(7) d. premature
(8) a. drearily
(9) c. venture
(10) d. abject
(11) d. traversed
(12) b. disconsolate

VII.2 Find & Rephrase
Answers may vary. Suggested answers:

(1) repulsion
- a. I once saw him, and shared

your feeling of repulsion
- b. I once saw him, and shared your feeling of disgust

(2) presence
- a. I feel as if the presence of a friend might do him good
- b. I feel as if the company of a friend might do him good

(3) premature
- a. full of premature twilight
- b. full of early twilight

(4) mien
- a. an infinite sadness of mien
- b. an infinite sadness of expression

(5) disconsolate
- a. like some disconsolate prisoner
- b. like some miserable prisoner

VII.3 Words & Meanings in Context
(1) d. dare
(2) d. expression
(3) b. stimulating
(4) d. disgust
(5) c. company
(6) b. blood flow
(7) c. early
(8) a. stark
(9) a. movements
(10) a. crossed
(11) a. miserable
(12) d. bleakly

Unit VIII: The Last Night

VIII.1 Definitions Completion
(1) C
(2) O
(3) M
(4) E
(5) I
(6) J
(7) L
(8) K
(9) B
(10) N
(11) G
(12) F
(13) H
(14) D
(15) A

VIII.2 Cloze Test
(1) termination
(2) peevishly
(3) wrack

(4) foul play
(5) lumber
(6) lawny
(7) induce
(8) unseemly
(9) resolution
(10) get this through hands
(11) diaphanous
(12) lamentation
(13) made away with
(14) hold water
(15) doggedly

VIII.3 Synonyms
(1) improper
(2) deal with this
(3) jumble
(4) will power
(5) soft
(6) irritably
(7) criminal violence
(8) concluding statement
(9) make sense
(10) weeping
(11) murdered
(12) determinedly
(13) fine
(14) cloud
(15) persuade

VIII.4 Matching Words to Meanings
(1) criminal = malefactor
(2) clouds = scud
(3) devout = pious
(4) seeds = kernels
(5) revenge = vengeance
(6) unreasonable = exorbitant
(7) twisted = contorted
(8) discernment = penetration
(9) fire iron = poker
(10) paleness = pallor
(11) irreligious statements = blasphemies
(12) small glass bottle = phial
(13) illnesses = maladies
(14) appearance = semblance
(15) blotchy = mottled

VIII.5 Word Webs
Answers will vary.

Possible Answers for "contorted":
- *Event(s): The discovery of Hyde's dead body*
- *Character(s): Hyde/Jekyll (dead); Utterson; Poole*
- *Location(s): Dr Jekyll's cabinet*
- *Theme(s): transformation; the*

supernatural; duality; death
- *Context(s): Victorian attitudes to suicide*
- *Quote(s): "the body of a man [...] still twitching"; "life was quite gone"*
- *Motif(s)/Symbol(s): physical deformity*

Possible Answers for "semblance":
- *Event(s): The discovery of Hyde's dead body*
- *Character(s): Hyde/Jekyll (dead); Utterson; Poole*
- *Location(s): Dr Jekyll's cabinet*
- *Theme(s): hypocrisy; lies; appearance vs reality*
- *Context(s): Gothic literature & its conventions*
- *Quote(s): "the cords of his face still moved"*
- *Motif(s)/Symbol(s): faces*

Possible Answers for "phial":
- *Event(s): The manner of Hyde's death*
- *Character(s): Hyde/Jekyll (dead); Utterson; Poole*
- *Location(s): Dr Jekyll's cabinet*
- *Theme(s): metamorphosis; the supernatural; exterior vs interior*
- *Context(s): Science & Religion in the Victorian Age*
- *Quote(s): "the strong smell of kernels"*
- *Motif(s)/Symbol(s): potion*

VIII.6 Words & Meanings in Context
(1) c. fire iron
(2) c. small glass bottle
(3) c. appearance
(4) b. criminal
(5) d. clouds
(6) b. illnesses
(7) b. discernment
(8) a. unreasonable
(9) a. devout
(10) d. blotchy
(11) c. paleness
(12) a. revenge
(13) a. irreligious statements

Unit IX: Dr Lanyon's Narrative

IX.1 Matching Words to Meanings
(1) added = appended
(2) peculiar = idiosyncratic
(3) state = posture
(4) confusion = farrago
(5) unstable = flighty
(6) physical strength = constitution
(7) restricted = constrained
(8) strong-smelling = pungent
(9) dreadful = morbid
(10) triggered = whetted
(11) a horse-drawn carriage used as a taxi = hansom
(12) obstacle = impediment
(13) conversation = intercourse
(14) goose pimples = incipient rigour
(15) utmost = capital

IX.2 Cloze Test
(1) hansom
(2) constitution
(3) farrago
(4) constrained
(5) impediment
(6) whetted
(7) idiosyncratic
(8) incipient rigour
(9) capital
(10) posture
(11) appended
(12) pungent
(13) intercourse
(14) morbid
(15) flighty

IX.3 Synonyms
(1) conversation
(2) unstable
(3) strong-smelling
(4) dreadful
(5) a horse-drawn carriage used as a taxi
(6) confusion
(7) restricted
(8) goose pimples
(9) obstacle
(10) state
(11) utmost
(12) triggered
(13) physical strength
(14) peculiar
(15) added

IX.4 Definitions Assessment
(1) True
(2) True
(3) True
(4) False
(5) False
(6) False
(7) True
(8) False
(9) False
(10) False
(11) True
(12) True
(13) True
(14) False
(15) True

IX.5 Find & Rephrase
Answers may vary. Suggested answers:

(1) pang
- a. conscious at his touch of a certain icy <u>pang</u> along my blood
- b. conscious at his touch of a certain icy <u>sensation</u> along my blood
(2) civilly
- a. he replied <u>civilly</u> enough
- b. he replied <u>politely</u> enough
(3) convulsive
- a. the <u>convulsive</u> action of his jaws
- b. the <u>violent</u> action of his jaws
(4) minims
- a. measured out a few <u>minims</u> of the red tincture
- b. measured out a few <u>drops</u> of the red tincture
(5) effervesce
- a. to <u>effervesce</u> audibly
- b. to <u>fizz</u> audibly

IX.6 Words & Meanings in Context
(1) c. depravity
(2) d. wonder
(3) c. discussion
(4) d. desperate
(5) b. preternatural
(6) a. difference
(7) a. contemptible
(8) b. drops
(9) d. bubbling
(10) c. politely
(11) b. outfit
(12) a. violent
(13) d. transformations

Unit X: Dr Jekyll's Full Statement Of The Case

X.1 Definitions Completion
(1) G
(2) L
(3) T
(4) M
(5) O
(6) J
(7) B
(8) A
(9) S
(10) D
(11) R
(12) F
(13) N
(14) P
(15) H
(16) C
(17) K
(18) E
(19) Q
(20) I

X.2 Cloze Test
(1) endowed
(2) inveterately
(3) radically
(4) aura
(5) aspirations
(6) duplicity
(7) denizens
(8) extraneous
(9) faggots
(10) exacting
(11) trench
(12) attired
(13) gaiety
(14) polity
(15) agents
(16) blazoned
(17) effulgence
(18) infallibly
(19) degradation
(20) excellent parts

X.3 Synonyms
(1) liveliness
(2) people
(3) outstanding qualities
(4) boasted
(5) group
(6) separate
(7) hopes
(8) demanding
(9) components
(10) substances

(11) habitually
(12) clothed
(13) division
(14) blessed
(15) fundamentally
(16) brilliance
(17) inevitably
(18) distinctive quality
(19) deceitfulness
(20) shame

X.4 Definitions Assessment
(1) True
(2) False
(3) False
(4) False
(5) False
(6) True
(7) False
(8) False
(9) True
(10) True
(11) False
(12) False
(13) True
(14) True
(15) False
(16) False
(17) False
(18) True
(19) False
(20) True

X.5 Find & Rephrase
Answers may vary. Suggested answers:

(1) vigilance
• a. their unsleeping <u>vigilance</u>
• b. their unsleeping <u>watchfulness</u>
(2) efficacy
• a. I had now transferred the stamping <u>efficacy</u>
• b. I had now transferred the stamping <u>power</u>
(3) repugnance
• a. I was conscious of no <u>repugnance</u>
• b. I was conscious of no <u>disgust</u>
(4) dissolution
• a. once more suffered the pangs of <u>dissolution</u>
• b. once more suffered the pangs of <u>change</u>
(5) diabolical
• a. it was neither <u>diabolical</u> nor divine
• b. it was neither <u>satanic</u> nor divine

X.6 Words & Meanings in Context
(1) d. inconsistency
(2) a. unprincipled
(3) d. soul
(4) b. watchfulness
(5) b. torrent
(6) a. fend off
(7) c. thugs
(8) c. small amount
(9) c. second-hand
(10) b. agonising
(11) b. wickedness
(12) a. financial
(13) c. power

X.7 Matching Words to Meanings
(1) relish = gusto
(2) putting forth = projecting
(3) uncontrolled = unbridled
(4) intrinsically = inherently
(5) violent spasms = throes
(6) colluded = connived
(7) evil = malign
(8) tendency = propensity
(9) demon = familiar
(10) swarthy = swart
(11) savaged = mauled
(12) dissecting room = anatomical theatre
(13) pleasing = comely
(14) mental powers = faculties
(15) punishment = chastisement
(16) craftily = insidiously
(17) cause for anger = provocation
(18) agonize = suffer
(19) destroy = obliterate
(20) temptations = inducements

X.8 Cloze Test
(1) chastisement
(2) connived
(3) faculties
(4) suffer
(5) inherently
(6) inducements
(7) malign
(8) throes
(9) provocation
(10) comely
(11) unbridled
(12) projecting
(13) mauled
(14) familiar
(15) propensity
(16) gusto
(17) anatomical theatre
(18) obliterate
(19) swart
(20) insidiously

X.9 Synonyms
(1) agonize
(2) tendency
(3) savaged
(4) mental powers
(5) demon
(6) cause for anger
(7) craftily
(8) intrinsically
(9) swarthy
(10) temptations
(11) pleasing
(12) evil
(13) colluded
(14) dissecting room
(15) destroy
(16) uncontrolled
(17) violent spasms
(18) putting forth
(19) punishment
(20) relish

X.10 Definitions Assessment
(1) True
(2) False
(3) False
(4) True
(5) False
(6) False
(7) True
(8) False
(9) False
(10) False
(11) True
(12) False
(13) True
(14) False
(15) False
(16) True
(17) False
(18) False
(19) True
(20) True

X.11 Antonyms
A. condescension
B. delirium
C. usurp
D. renunciation
E. self-indulgence
F. abhorrence
G. succumbed
H. vainglorious
I. amorphous
J. languidly

X.12 Words & Meanings in Context

(1) c. surrendered
(2) b. forsaking
(3) a. unshaped
(4) d. sickly
(5) d. warning
(6) c. exhaustion
(7) b. slavishly
(8) c. wretched
(9) a. overly proud
(10) d. supplant
(11) b. scorn
(12) b. send
(13) d. derangement

Vocabulary Scavenger Hunt Challenges

I: Story Of The Door
A. walking noisily and stiffly = stumping
B. an intersecting or connecting street = a cross street
C. A single word used to indicate an exclamation = halloa
D. A simile used to describe an undemonstrative disposition = as emotional as a bagpipe
E. to ruin a person's reputation = make his name stink
F. a person's reputation = credit
G. A simile that draws on figures from Greek mythology = as wild as harpies
H. to gain financially = to make capital
I. desired to resist = liked to stick out
J. a large, unspecified amount of money = The figure was stiff

II: Search For Mr Hyde
A. A simile that draws on dancing = as clean as a ballroom floor
B. A metaphor that compares London to an animal = low growl of London
C. 3 consecutive words that combine low and steady sounds with rattling sounds = hum and clatter
D. became greater in intensity = swelled
E. A metaphor that draws on serpents = a hissing intake
F. quite determinedly = pretty

fixedly
G. appropriate speech = fitting language
H. a deadly combination = murderous mixture
I. barely mortal = hardly human
J. 2 consecutive sibilant words that emphasise the presence of evil = Satan's signature

III: Dr Jekyll Was Quite At Ease
A. a large indefinite number = scores
B. to hold a person back / to claim a person's attention = detain
C. becoming clear-headed = sobering their minds
D. ability = capacity
E. harboured = cherished
F. the second of two things mentioned = latter
G. an attentive onlooker = A close observer
H. dismissed (something) casually = carried it off gaily
I. without compassion or pity = ruthlessly
J. a darkening facial expression = there came a blackness about his eyes

IV: The Carew Murder Case
A. thought / reflection = musing
B. approaching = drawing near
C. were close enough to talk = had come within speech
D. became pregnant OR formed = conceived
E. behaving (informal) = carrying on
F. An animal simile = ape-like fury
G. A 4-word metaphor comparing physical assault to a severe weather event = a storm of blows
H. the low area at the side of a street to carry off water = gutter
I. A single old-fashioned word meaning to where = whither
J. something will be much talked about = This will make a deal of noise

V: Incident Of The Letter
A. precisely = nicely
B. kept in the dark = unsunned
C. A metaphor that draws on the

idea of a resting bird = The fog still slept on the wing
D. 4 consecutive words that form a simile AND which are alliterative = lamps glimmered like carbuncles
E. A single obsolete word meaning dissolved = resolved
F. to thin out and make disappear – disperse
G. gradually = Insensibly
H. relaxed = melted
I. helpful = obliging
J. determine his subsequent actions = shape his future course

VI: Incident Of Dr Lanyon
A. barring = exclusion
B. unable to be changed = incurable
C. from this point on = henceforth
D. An example of parallelism = I am the chief of sinners, I am the chief of sufferers
E. emasculating = unmanning
F. to ease = to lighten
G. An example of personification that draws on sadness = a melancholy candle
H. written on the cover / outside of something = superscribed
I. joined = bracketted
J. duties = obligations

VII: Incident At The Window
A. a fool = ass
B. discovered = found it out
C. yard = court
D. hope = trust
E. An example of repetition = very low [...] very low
F. go for a brisk walk = take a quick turn
G. the rooms are a mess = the place is really not fit
H. erased / removed = was struck out of
I. a momentary view = glimpse
J. corresponding = answering

VIII: The Last Night
A. complete / utter = mere
B. dismayed / shocked = appalled
C. loud noise = riot
D. followed – succeeded
E. 3 examples of personification in a single sentence = the quiet

lamplight / fire [...] chattering / the
kettle singing
F. ordinary = commonplace
G. severely = sorely
H. gazed upon = beheld
I. a suicide = self-destroyer
J. final judgement = account

IX: Dr Lanyon's Narrative
A. feigning = affecting
B. calmness = coolness
C. incapable of being accounted
for = inexplicable
D. promises = vows
E. ridiculed / scorned = derided
F. An example of a tricolon (i.e.
rule of 3) = reeled, staggered,
clutched
G. blood-shot = injected
H. A simile that draws on
resurrection = like a man restored
from death
I. sceptical = incredulous
J. sorrow for faults or sins =
penitence

X: Dr Jekyll's Full Statement Of The Case
A. signalled the approach of =
heralded
B. bring back to an original or
former state = recall
C. imminent terrible fate =
impending doom
D. A metaphor that draws on heat
and water = a soul boiling with
causeless hatreds
E. a joint inheritor = co-heir
F. made motions while speaking =
gesticulated
G. rebellious = insurgent
H. An animal simile = ape-like
tricks
I. destroyed himself = ruined
himself
J. submission to hopelessness =
acquiescence of despair

Complete Words & Meanings By Chapter

STORY OF THE DOOR

rugged: stony
countenance: face
dusty: uninteresting
eminently: extremely
beaconed: shone
austere: strict
mortify: suppress
vintages: expensive wines
heresy: unconventional opinion
chambers: office
catholicity: broad-mindedness
kinsman: relative
singularly: distinctly
chanced: happened
rambles: walks
emulously: competitively
in coquetry: attractively
thoroughfare: road
florid: flamboyant
passage: customers
passenger: pedestrian
gable: upper triangular-shaped part of a wall
distained: discoloured
mouldings: decorations
ravages: damage
cane: walking stick
Juggernaut: unstoppable force
collared: grabbed
Sawbones: doctor
apothecary: doctor
harpies: angry women
screwed: forced
apocryphal: doubtful
proprieties: respectability
capers: mischief
vein: mood
delicacy: reluctance
partakes too much of: has too much in common with
Queer Street: financial difficulties
pedantically: excessively

SEARCH FOR MR HYDE

dry: dull
divinity: religious writer
endorsed: marked
holograph: handwritten
decease: death
benefactor: financial supporter
burthen: burden
eyesore: irritant
hitherto: previously
attributes: qualities
baffled: perturbed
presentment: appearance
fiend: devil
obnoxious: offensive
citadel: fortress
dapper: well-dressed
boisterous: lively
decided: determined
geniality: friendliness
reposed: was based
fanciful: irrational
balderdash: nonsense
estranged: alienated
Damon and Pythias: loyal friends
conveyancing: transferring ownership
composure: calmness
protégé: student
besieged: overwhelmed
dwelling: house
gross: total
bidding: commands
inordinate: excessive
bondage: enslavement
bowels of mercy: tenderness
concourse: crowdedness
quaint: odd
footfalls: footsteps
arrested: attracted
prevision: prediction
apropos: given this
disquietude: uneasiness
perplexity: confusion
malformation: abnormality
timidity: lack of confidence
troglodytic: primitive
transpires: shines
transfigures: transforms
clay continent: human body

fanlight: window
flags: flagstones
cabinets: cupboards
wont: accustomed
dissecting room: anatomy theatre
statute of limitations: time limit
pede claudo: on limping foot (i.e. delayed)
condoned: accepted
brooded: dwelled
iniquity: immoral behaviour
apprehension: anxiety
conceived: formed

gin palace: pub
umber: dark (brown) pigment
blackguardly: disreputable
hypocrisy: insincerity
odious: unpleasant
napery: household linen
connoisseur: expert judge
ransacked: searched
hearth: fireplace
disinterred: unearthed
familiars: friends
fugitive: runaway

DR JEKYLL WAS QUITE AT EASE

cronies: friends
contrived: arranged
loose-tongued: talkative
threshold: doorstep
unobtrusive: restrained
hide-bound: conservative
pedant: purist
blatant: unashamed
a trifle: a little
abominable: loathsome
incoherency of manner: hysteria
make a clean breast of: confess
downright: absolutely
irrepressible: uncontrollable

INCIDENT OF THE LETTER

anatomical: relating to the body
quarters: accommodation
gaunt: empty
cupola: domed skylight
baize: woollen cloth
cabinet: small private room
presses: cupboards
cheval glass: upright tilting mirror
ruminated: thought
signified: stated
qualm: fit
circulars: advertisements
oration: speech
eddy: whirlpool
ticklish: difficult
carbuncles: red gems
imperial: reddish-purple
counsel: the law
elicited: generated
sedulously: meticulously

THE CAREW MURDER CASE

singular: exceptional
rendered: made
accosted: approached
trifling: playing
brandishing: waving
mangled: injured
insensate: senseless
whither: where
quailed: recoiled
stature: height
pall: dark cloud
routing: blowing away
hues: colours
lurid: intense
conflagration: fire
slatternly: scruffy
kindled: lit
assail: attack

INCIDENT OF DR LANYON

resented: regarded negatively
ken: knowledge
unearthed: uncovered
disreputable: scandalous
callous: cold-hearted
blotted out: erased
seclusion: isolation
death warrant: death sentence
accursed: damned
drift: meaning
suffer: allow
amities: friendships

tenor: direction
trustee: executor
stringent: strict
disquieted: uneasy
bondage: imprisonment
inscrutable: enigmatic
recluse: hermit
fell off: decreased

INCIDENT AT THE WINDOW

repulsion: disgust
presence: company
premature: early
mien: expression
disconsolate: miserable
drearily: bleakly
whipping up: stimulating
circulation: blood flow
venture: dare
abject: stark
traversed: crossed
stirrings: movements

THE LAST NIGHT

doggedly: determinedly
foul play: criminal violence
wrack: cloud
diaphanous: fine
lawny: soft
peevishly: irritably
unseemly: improper
lamentation: weeping
get this through hands: deal with this
termination: concluding statement
lumber: jumble
resolution: will power
made away with: murdered
induce: persuade
hold water: make sense
maladies: illnesses
exorbitant: unreasonable
mottled: blotchy
pallor: paleness
poker: fire iron
vengeance: revenge
malefactor: criminal
scud: clouds
contorted: twisted

semblance: appearance
phial: small glass bottle
kernels: seeds
pious: devout
blasphemies: irreligious statements
penetration: discernment

DR LANYON'S NARRATIVE

intercourse: conversation
morbid: dreadful
capital: utmost
farrago: confusion
hansom: a horse-drawn carriage used as a taxi
pungent: strong-smelling
appended: added
whetted: triggered
flighty: unstable
impediment: obstacle
posture: state
constrained: restricted
constitution: physical strength
incipient rigour: goose pimples
idiosyncratic: peculiar
accoutrement: outfit
misbegotten: contemptible
disparity: difference
sombre: desperate
pang: sensation
civilly: politely
convulsive: violent
minims: drops
effervesce: fizz
ebullition: bubbling
metamorphoses: transformations
parley: discussion
prodigy: wonder
transcendental: preternatural
turpitude: depravity

DR JEKYLL'S FULL STATEMENT OF THE CASE

endowed: blessed
excellent parts: outstanding qualities
gaiety: liveliness
duplicity: deceitfulness
blazoned: boasted
exacting: demanding
aspirations: hopes

degradation: shame
trench: division
inveterately: habitually
polity: group
denizens: people
infallibly: inevitably
radically: fundamentally
extraneous: separate
faggots: components
attired: clothed
agents: substances
aura: distinctive quality
effulgence: brilliance
scruple: small amount
immaterial tabernacle: soul
racking: agonising
recklessness: rashness
millrace: torrent
exulting: glorying
constellations: stars
vigilance: watchfulness
efficacy: power
repugnance: disgust
dissolution: change
diabolical: satanic
aversions: distaste
incoherency: inconsistency
unscrupulous: unprincipled
parry: fend off
pecuniary: financial
bravos: thugs
vicarious: second-hand
depravity: wickedness
familiar: demon
inherently: intrinsically
malign: evil
insidiously: craftily
connived: colluded
chastisement: punishment
comely: pleasing
swart: swarthy
anatomical theatre: dissecting room
projecting: putting forth
gusto: relish
faculties: mental powers
suffer: agonize
inducements: temptations
obliterate: destroy
throes: violent spasms
unbridled: uncontrolled

propensity: tendency
provocation: cause for anger
mauled: savaged
delirium: derangement
self-indulgence: unrestrained self-gratification
rent: ripped
renunciation: forsaking
condescension: scorn
vainglorious: overly proud
quarry: prey
succumbed: surrendered
consign: send
rifle: ransack
obsequiously: slavishly
abhorrence: loathing
the gallows: execution by hanging
prostration: exhaustion
premonitory: warning
languidly: sickly
poignant: wretched
amorphous: unshaped
usurp: supplant
scaffold: platform for execution

abhorrence: loathing
abject: stark
abominable: loathsome
accosted: approached
accoutrement: outfit
accursed: damned
agents: substances
amities: friendships
amorphous: unshaped
anatomical: relating to the body
anatomical theatre: dissecting room
apocryphal: doubtful
apothecary: doctor
appended: added
apprehension: anxiety
apropos: given this
arrested: attracted
aspirations: hopes
assail: attack
a trifle: a little
attired: clothed
attributes: qualities
aura: distinctive quality
austere: strict
aversions: distaste

baffled: perturbed
baize: woollen cloth
balderdash: nonsense
beaconed: shone
benefactor: financial supporter
besieged: overwhelmed
bidding: commands
blackguardly: disreputable
blasphemies: irreligious statements
blatant: unashamed
blazoned: boasted
blotted out: erased
boisterous: lively
bondage: enslavement
bondage: imprisonment
bowels of mercy: tenderness
brandishing: waving

bravos: thugs
brooded: dwelled
burthen: burden

cabinet: small private room
cabinets: cupboards
callous: cold-hearted
cane: walking stick
capers: mischief
capital: utmost
carbuncles: red gems
catholicity: broad-mindedness
chambers: office
chanced: happened
chastisement: punishment
cheval glass: upright tilting mirror
circulars: advertisements
circulation: blood flow
citadel: fortress
civilly: politely
clay continent: human body
collared: grabbed
comely: pleasing
composure: calmness
conceived: formed
concourse: crowdedness
condescension: scorn
condoned: accepted
conflagration: fire
connived: colluded
connoisseur: expert judge
consign: send
constellations: stars
constitution: physical strength
constrained: restricted
contorted: twisted
contrived: arranged
conveyancing: transferring ownership
convulsive: violent
counsel: the law
countenance: face
cronies: friends
cupola: domed skylight

Damon and Pythias: loyal friends
dapper: well-dressed
death warrant: death sentence

decease: death
decided: determined
degradation: shame
delicacy: reluctance
delirium: derangement
denizens: people
depravity: wickedness
diabolical: satanic
diaphanous: fine
disconsolate: miserable
disinterred: unearthed
disparity: difference
disquieted: uneasy
disquietude: uneasiness
disreputable: scandalous
dissecting room: anatomy theatre
dissolution: change
distained: discoloured
divinity: religious writer
doggedly: determinedly
downright: absolutely
drearily: bleakly
drift: meaning
dry: dull
duplicity: deceitfulness
dusty: uninteresting
dwelling: house

ebullition: bubbling
eddy: whirlpool
effervesce: fizz
efficacy: power
effulgence: brilliance
elicited: generated
eminently: extremely
emulously: competitively
endorsed: marked
endowed: blessed
estranged: alienated
exacting: demanding
excellent parts: outstanding qualities
exorbitant: unreasonable
extraneous: separate
exulting: glorying
eyesore: irritant

faculties: mental powers

faggots: components
familiar: demon
familiars: friends
fanciful: irrational
fanlight: window
farrago: confusion
fell off: decreased
fiend: devil
flags: flagstones
flighty: unstable
florid: flamboyant
footfalls: footsteps
foul play: criminal violence
fugitive: runaway

gable: upper triangular-shaped part of a wall
gaiety: liveliness
gaunt: empty
geniality: friendliness
get this through hands: deal with this
gin palace: pub
gross: total
gusto: relish

hansom: a horse-drawn carriage used as a taxi
harpies: angry women
hearth: fireplace
heresy: unconventional opinion
hide-bound: conservative
hitherto: previously
hold water: make sense
holograph: handwritten
hues: colours
hypocrisy: insincerity

idiosyncratic: peculiar
immaterial tabernacle: soul
impediment: obstacle
imperial: reddish-purple
incipient rigour: goose pimples
incoherency: inconsistency
incoherency of manner: hysteria
in coquetry: attractively
induce: persuade
inducements: temptations
infallibly: inevitably

inherently: intrinsically
iniquity: immoral behaviour
inordinate: excessive
inscrutable: enigmatic
insensate: senseless
insidiously: craftily
intercourse: conversation
inveterately: habitually
irrepressible: uncontrollable

Juggernaut: unstoppable force

ken: knowledge
kernels: seeds
kindled: lit
kinsman: relative

lamentation: weeping
languidly: sickly
lawny: soft
loose-tongued: talkative
lumber: jumble
lurid: intense

made away with: murdered
make a clean breast of: confess
maladies: illnesses
malefactor: criminal
malformation: abnormality
malign: evil
mangled: injured
mauled: savaged
metamorphoses: transformations
mien: expression
millrace: torrent
minims: drops
misbegotten: contemptible
morbid: dreadful
mortify: suppress
mottled: blotchy
mouldings: decorations

napery: household linen

obliterate: destroy
obnoxious: offensive
obsequiously: slavishly

odious: unpleasant
oration: speech

pall: dark cloud
pallor: paleness
pang: sensation
parley: discussion
parry: fend off
partakes too much of: has too much in common with
passage: customers
passenger: pedestrian
pecuniary: financial
pedant: purist
pedantically: excessively
pede claudo: on limping foot (i.e. delayed)
peevishly: irritably
penetration: discernment
perplexity: confusion
phial: small glass bottle
pious: devout
poignant: wretched
poker: fire iron
polity: group
posture: state
premature: early
premonitory: warning
presence: company
presentment: appearance
presses: cupboards
prevision: prediction
prodigy: wonder
projecting: putting forth
propensity: tendency
proprieties: respectability
prostration: exhaustion
protégé: student
provocation: cause for anger
pungent: strong-smelling

quailed: recoiled
quaint: odd
qualm: fit
quarry: prey
quarters: accommodation
Queer Street: financial difficulties

racking: agonising
radically: fundamentally
rambles: walks
ransacked: searched
ravages: damage
recklessness: rashness
recluse: hermit
rendered: made
rent: ripped
renunciation: forsaking
reposed: was based
repugnance: disgust
repulsion: disgust
resented: regarded negatively
resolution: will power
rifle: ransack
routing: blowing away
rugged: stony
ruminated: thought

Sawbones: doctor
scaffold: platform for execution
screwed: forced
scruple: small amount
scud: clouds
seclusion: isolation
sedulously: meticulously
self-indulgence: unrestrained self-
gratification
semblance: appearance
signified: stated
singular: exceptional
singularly: distinctly
slatternly: scruffy
sombre: desperate
stature: height
statute of limitations: time limit
stirrings: movements
stringent: strict
succumbed: surrendered
suffer: agonize
suffer: allow
swart: swarthy

tenor: direction
termination: concluding statement
the gallows: execution by hanging

thoroughfare: road
threshold: doorstep
throes: violent spasms
ticklish: difficult
timidity: lack of confidence
transcendental: preternatural
transfigures: transforms
transpires: shines
traversed: crossed
trench: division
trifling: playing
troglodytic: primitive
trustee: executor
turpitude: depravity

umber: dark (brown) pigment
unbridled: uncontrolled
unearthed: uncovered
unobtrusive: restrained
unscrupulous: unprincipled
unseemly: improper
usurp: supplant

vainglorious: overly proud
vein: mood
vengeance: revenge
venture: dare
vicarious: second-hand
vigilance: watchfulness
vintages: expensive wines

whetted: triggered
whipping up: stimulating
whither: where
wont: accustomed
wrack: cloud

Printed in Great Britain
by Amazon

16828387R00061